The Melanin Empath

DISCOVER THE KNOWLEDGE OF MELANTED BEINGS BORN WITH EMPATH ENERGY

GW00776315

Jade Asikiwe

© 2019

THIS COLLECTION INCLUDES THE FOLLOWING BOOKS:

Melanin: Gift of the Cosmos

The Power of an Empath & Natural Healer for Beginners

TABLE OF CONTENTS

MELANIN: GIFT OF THE COSMOS

INTRODUCTION

What is it about the sun that comforts us in a way similar to none? That natural force that awakens you from unconscious. Those warm sunrays piercing the sky, gleaming down on your body in a positive frequency. That natural calm that occurs when you take a moment to appreciate the universe as you raise self-awareness. The cool breeze that passes over your shoulder and puts you at ease with your surroundings. We are creatures of light, love and peace. Within us lies the information of the universe, a sweet sacred element known as melanin.

Melanin has numerous health benefits for the body, but it also exists on a cosmic level. This sacred element is found in small amounts in every creation, even inanimate objects. People who possess concentrated amounts of melanin are advantaged when exposed to the sun. Melanated beings are vibrant creatures deeply rooted in the cosmos, known for living in harmony with nature, they are the original beings of the Earth.

Melanin is a chemical produced by the pineal gland of the brain. Through autopsies performed on deceased soldiers during the Vietnam War, it was learned that the pineal gland of the brain is larger in African Americans. The darker pigment of skin is a result of the melanin- but many more discoveries are known.

Melanin exists as a powerful spiritual energy. It is much more than just the pigment of one's skin color; melanin is also the core fundamental unit that makes up the entirety of the universe. It emits and absorbs energy, works in the brain and digest information from sunlight. Melanin makes you more receptive to all the energy sources on the light spectrum, much more than a person lacking this element. This is because the color white is naturally reflective and pushes away all light while black, the color of melanin, absorbs all light.

It is this ability to absorb and see the entire spectrum of light that makes melanated beings unique. By seeing and emitting all the lights on the spectrum, they access heightened creativity and knowledge of the universe. Recent studies have shown that light actually carries within it intelligent information. When you receive sunlight, you are essentially downloading and converting new information from the universe. You can charge this energy and help it flow, while giving you greater ideas and enlightened perspective. Melanin, therefore, is a driving power of the universe and connects to us all both physically and energetically.

As you read this book, you will unlock the knowledge to increase and understand your identity. You will learn how to increase the melanin contained in your body and exponentially, your abilities to attract what you desire in life. You will also learn about what to avoid in regards of nutrition and how melanin exists on a cosmic level.

Enjoy! Keep your mind open to the pure, fulfilling life that you can lead as you learn the key components of light, love and energy.

Chapter 1: What is Melanin?

Most people know melanin only as its physical manifestation, as it is the presence of melanin within a person that determines how light or dark their skin tone is. However, it is also much more. It is the dark matter present in every being in the universe, existing on even a cellular level. It is the core unit of existence with the power to emit and absorb energy. It also improves digestive function, vision, and the inner workings of the brain. Produced by the pineal gland, it is still found in every organ in the human body, flowing through the blood and being present in every subatomic particle of the body.

The purest form of melanin is black because it absorbs all colors. It is found in the eyes, hair and skin of people of African descent in varying degrees. The darker that the melanin is, the more concentrated it has taken form.

Melanin: What Does it Mean?

Melanin, like most words, can be broken down into its origins to form an understanding of the full term.

The first part of the word, 'MEL' is derived from the Greek word Melano, which means black. 'ANIN' is derived from the word Amine, which describes a functional group with a nitrogen base and additional hydrocarbons. By definition, therefore, melanin means 'black amine.'

This definition makes sense because melanin is black in its purest form. This is because melanin works like any other thing seen by the human eye. For the human eye to see color, it is captured as reflections from light. Only when light is reflected from the surface of an object or a being will there be color. When a surface has no color and reflects no light, it appears black in color. Melanin cells, when in their purest form, have absorbed a large amount of energy. Since melanin never loses that energy once it becomes pure, it will always remain black.

Now, it has been described that melanin is black in its purest form. But what about when it is not pure? Melanin is a pigment. As a pigment, it has varying shades that can exist in the human body. Melanin can be tinted anywhere on the spectrum from yellow to pure black. It is most often yellow-tinted in Caucasian and Asian people and exists in its purest form in those with a dark skin color and a rich African heritage.

ABOUT PINEAL AND MELANIN (

THE SCIENCE)

Interestingly melanin absorbs all types of energy such as sunlight, electromagnetic, music heard by the human ear and sounds the human ear cannot hear, phone waves, radio waves, radar, computer radiation, x-ray, cosmic rays, ultraviolet rays, heat waves, microwaves, etc. Very similar to the expression, *"You are what you eat and listen to"*. Melanin uses the energy in the entire universe such as water energy, earth, moon, sun, galaxy, cycles of planets, cycles of minerals etc. On the molecular level the melanin particles called electrons, protons, neutrons and solitons rearrange their orbit. This is called resonance. In other words, the melanin particles vibrate and rearrange themselves to fill the weak (low) energy sites. Resonance causes a particle to move, this movement causes a small gap (low energy) site and the other particles rearrange themselves to (double bond shift) fill the gap.

Melanin is the natural chemical that makes Black people's skin Black. It is present in Black people's bodies, skin, cells, nerves, brain, muscles, bones, reproductive and digestive systems and all bodily functions in a higher amount than all other races.

Melanin is a biological active substance of various size cells. It is made of nutrients such as indoles, histamines, phenylalanine, catecholamines (norepinephrine, epinephrine, dopamine, etc.) and the amino acid tyrosine. Melanin is made of various attached parts called chains which are linked to unsaturated carbon-carbon, saturated carbon-carbon, carbon-nitrogen, organometallic, ether. Peroxides and quinine which are brown to black in color. Chemicals such as Flavin, Pteridines, Flavonoid, Naphthoquinone, Polycyclic Quinone, Anthraquinone, Phenoxazine, convert into Melanin (polymerize or co-polymerize).

The color of melanin appears as black because it is absorbing all colors. Once the color enters the melanin it cannot escape. Melanin is concentrated colors, it is a cellular Black Hole similar to the Black

Holes in outer space. The human eye only sees colors that are reflected away from an object. If an object appears Black in color, that means that the object is absorbing all colors except Black. Black is reflected away from the object, consequently, you see Black. Black is a pigment (color) that makes carbon Black in appearance.

MELANIN ON A SCIENTIFIC LEVEL

Melanin is synthesized (produced) by the body when the chemical L-3, 4-dihydroxyphenylalanine is catalyzed by tyrosine. The amino acid tyrosine is the key to this process. Tyrosine is both produced by the body and can be supplemented with pills or naturally by increasing the intake of certain foods. It is found in unique cells called melanocytes. Inside these melanocytes are vesicles called melanosomes, where tiny granules of the pigment melanin can be found.

Over time, the melanosomes detach themselves from the melanocytes, moving through the body and to other cells and eventually making their way to the epidermal cells. These are the cells found in the two topmost layers of your skin and the concentration and distribution of the melanin pigment determines how light or dark your skin appears. Melanin also absorbs light from a scientific viewpoint, but not in the same way that is known to exist in the cosmos. The darker color absorbs light and protects the DNA of the body from the harmful ultraviolet rays from the sun.

Though melanin exists throughout the body, it is concentrated in several key areas. It is found predominantly in hair, skin, the irises (pupils) of the eyes, the locus coeruleus and substantia nigra of the brain, the stria vascularis of the inner ear, and the zona reticularis and medulla of the adrenal gland. There are three major types of melanin in the body, each playing a specific role.

• <u>Eumelanin, which is found only in small amounts. These small amounts can do things like make hair blonde in color.</u>

• <u>Pheomelanin, which is found in the skin and hair. This melanin may give red and pink colors to red-haired people. Though it is darker than eumelanin, it is not as protective against ultraviolet radiation.</u>

• <u>Neuromelanin, which is found throughout the brain. Deficiencies in neuromelanin may cause many types of neurological disorders.</u>

Though you may find scientists who ignore the incredible information that can be derived from an abundance of melanin, it cannot be denied that it exists in all bodies of each person on the planet. It is necessary for most bodily functions, comes in three different forms and must be present to help protect from cancer-causing ultraviolet radiation. The sun is not the enemy of the melanated being.

Melanin on a Cosmic Level

The scientific side of melanin has been established for many years, though for a long time scientists have believed it to be only a pigment to hair and skin color. The truth is that it plays many incredible roles in the body but the scientific definition only begins to scratch the surface. Melanin can also be described as a spiritual energy. It is incredibly powerful because while it can absorb light from all sides of the spectrum, it does not reflect much light. One way to think of melanin is as a partially-charged battery. This battery is always ready to accept and store more electrical charges. These electrical charges are energy, which can be created by focusing on and then storing things like sound and light.

There are four primary types of melanin that exist on a universal level. This includes planetary, cosmic, plant life (in the form of chlorophyll, including fungi and bacteria) and the animal kingdom (which we are a part of). As someone of African descent, you have rich melanin sources that exist in pure to near-pure form. In modern times, the larger amount of melanin found in Africans was not known about until the Vietnam War. When soldiers were killed during the war, they were shipped overseas to America before undergoing an autopsy to determine the cause of death. During these autopsies, the soldiers' brains were dissected. As scientists examined the brain, it was found that the pineal gland found in the brain of a Caucasian person was smaller than the pineal gland found in African soldiers.

Melanin and Ancient Egypt

A highly debated historical topic is what the skin color of Ancient Egyptians was. When people hear the term 'Egyptian,' some project it as a predominantly white society. Even though Egypt exists geographically in Africa, it is commonly believed that Egyptians are white, coming from North and South of the Sahara Desert and having differing skin tones that were lighter in nature. A major influencer of this opinion was a French scientist, Professor Pierre-Fernand Ceccaldi. In 1975, an unpreserved mummy was uncovered in Egypt. Ramesses II was flown to France, to be preserved by Professor Ceccaldi. The mummy of Ramesses had well-preserved hair, which was reddish in color. It was concluded that Ramesses II was a fair-skinned person that had ginger-colored hair. This discovery of this pigmentation heavily influenced the opinions of many scientists during the time, especially since there was not yet data that could disprove it. However, another theory in 2008 described the Egyptians as an incredibly diverse race, with its inhabitants coming from all over Africa. This would explain why the pigmentation of Ramesses was not representative of the entire race of Ancient Egypt.

Later in the 1970s, a group of scientists developed the Black Egyptian hypothesis. This hypothesis has since been adopted in the Afrocentric belief system, stating that Ancient Egypt was a society predominantly made up of melanated individuals. There are even some modern scholars that recognize this idea to an extent, agreeing that Nubians (indigenous Egyptian) and many Pharaohs had a black ancestral line. However, the beliefs under the Black Egyptian hypothesis claims that all of Egypt, from the northernmost to the southernmost parts of the country, was a black civilization. It is also believed that there are links to Sub-Saharan cultures that prove this relationship. Additionally, there are many individuals who existed during what is known as the Dynastic time period who were believed to be black, including notable men and women of history, including the inspiration for the Great Sphinx of Giza, King Tutankhamun and Cleopatra.

Today, there are still many scholars who support this idea, including Cheikh Anta Diop, Martin Bernal, Chancellor Williams, W.E.B. Du Bois, Segun Magbagbeola, Ivan van Sertima, and John G. Jackson. These scholars debated with others about the validity of the Black African hypothesis throughout the 20th century, with many of them using the descriptive terms 'Egyptian', 'African', and 'Black' interchangeably in their writing, research and speech. One of the most influential of these scholars was Cheikh Anta Diop, who used a multi-faceted approach to uncover the truth about the presence or lack thereof of melanin in the Ancient Egyptians. Diop tested skin samples from Egyptian mummies uncovered during the Mariette excavations by putting them under a microscope. Between the dermis and epidermis of the skin, melanin levels were tested and it was found that they were undeniably black. Diop also tested blood samples, finding that many of them had the 'B' blood type, which is most common in the African race. However, this research was not completely conclusive since the Egyptian samples were all from the same excavation site.

A 2017 study involved the extraction of DNA from 151 mummies of Egypt, uncovered in the Middle Egypt territory of Abusir el-Meleq. The DNA in these mummies were some of the first that were uncontaminated and completely intact. According to the age of the mummies, they lived during the time period of the late New Kingdom and the early Roman era, from the years 1388BCE to 146CE. They were able to uncover complete DNA for 90 of the mummies uncovered, which showed a similar profile during the entire period of time. Additionally, three of the mummies were analyzed to find Y-DNA, which is a common mitochondrial profile for North Africans and Middle Easterners. Even so, this single site still had a limited portrayal of all Ancient Egyptian life.

Another major proponent of this claim that all of Egypt was black is the intelligence of Ancient Egyptians. The Egyptians built the pyramids and are responsible for many of the inventions we have in today's society. Man has learned a lot from the life of the Ancient Egyptian. Many of the scholars supporting the Black Egyptian hypothesis believe they must be black because of the power of melanin. Already, it was known that the melanin caused darker skin pigmentation and did not just serve the purpose of determining skin tone. It was already known that melanin could absorb and exude a creative energy. This is shown through the ancient texts that describe the Egyptian's great machines, as well as their ability to fly in gliders, measure the distance from earth to the sun, and electroplate gold. Many other societies were overshadowed by the Ancient Egyptians as society spread, and the Egyptians became known as masters of magic like remote viewing, psychokinesis and precognition.

The final factor in the Black Egyptian hypothesis is the belief that all of civilization stemmed from the Ancient Egyptians. It is believed that they were the first human society created. The evidence behind this is the purity of some men and women of African descent. When a person of lighter skin tone has children with someone of a darker skin tone, it is impossible to keep that same purity of melanin. Therefore, it would only make sense that those of African descent were among the first living on earth, thus, the first Egyptians that walked the earth were black.

How Melanin Works as a Creative Power

Have you ever heard of techniques like positive thinking or positive visualization? These two techniques require the practicing individual to think about what they wish to bring into existence. They think of how they would like a situation to play out or what desires they have. The creative power of melanin, as you will see as you read through the book, works similar in this way. The abundance of melanin within your being allows you to attract the vibrations from the universe that align with the energy you are putting forth. Imagine for a moment that you desire inner peace and no longer stimulate from worldly desires . You would send out a positive, high vibration to attract that positive event that will lead to you advancing down that path.

You have probably heard the expression, 'like attracts like.' While this is not always true of people, it is always true of cosmic energy. The thoughts that you have and the way that you put forth your energy in the world attracts whatever you put out. If you continue to think that you will never be successful, that is what is going to happen. Instead, put out the positive vibe that you will find a solution. This solution will attract itself to your vibrational frequencies, bringing the ideas that you create into the physical world.

Chapter 2: The Many

Benefits of Melanin

Melanin is the black matter of all that exists. Even in the lightest beings, trace amounts of melanin are at work protecting their eyes and improving brain function. Melanin may even be considered the key to life itself, the solitary chemical involved in our being. Melanin has been found to be present in abundance during the moment of conception and as the embryo develops into what will be a child. This makes it an essential part of our lives, capable of manifesting itself not only on a physical level, but on a spiritual level. There are many benefits of melanin, both for our bodies and our spirits.

PHYSICAL BENEFITS OF MELANIN

#1: It is Necessary for Embryotic Development

Even from the moment of your conception, the dark matter melanin that is at the center of all in the universe protects you. It encases the egg and sperm as they join at the moment of conception, keeping them safe. Once you become an embryo, melanin works inside of that embryo, creating the products of the neural crest including nerve cells, brain cells and melanocytes. When an embryo is formed without enough melanin, it can lead to miscarriage or birth defects.

#2: Melanin Improves Brain Functions

Even when an individual does not possess the type of melanin that colors the skin, the black brain matter that is melanin still exists. This is necessary for primary brain functions, including motivational, emotional, motor and sensory activities. The greater the amount of melanin within the brain, the greater these (and other creative powers) are.

#3: It Slows the Aging Process

If you have ever compared the skin of an African American against the skin of someone with a lighter complexion of the same age, you may notice that the skin of those of African descent is usually smoother. This is because melanin protects from the damaging effects of UV rays from the sun. This prevents wrinkles and sun damage, promoting smooth, supple skin, even as you age.

#4: Heightened Melanin Levels Are Healing and Preventative

Melanin is a very healing substance, as it promotes cell regeneration and health throughout the body. The way that it protects cells allows it to lower the risk of cancers, especially melanoma. It also helps prevent genetic disorders, especially autoimmune disorders that cause the cells of the body to attack themselves. Finally, melanin repairs damaged tissue and both prevents and fights infections.

#6: It Protects from Damage of the Sun's Rays

Melanated individuals rarely burn from the sun- they simply absorb its energy. People may tan or become darker with sun exposure, which is the result of melanin being absorbed into the skin. People who are melanin recessive, however, may burn from being in the sun. Instead of protecting from damage, their skin reflects the light's rays and absorbs dangerous ultraviolet radiation. This is why it is important for individuals who have not been blessed with an abundance of melanin to use sunscreen and other methods to protect from harmful rays.

#7: Melanin Protects the Eyes

Eyes that are brown or black in color are covered in a coating of melanin. This melanin protects from sun damage, acting as natural sunglasses. When people who do not have melanated eyes look at sunlight, they may experience irritation or damage. Those with hazel, green, or blue eyes can have problems including irritation, burning, discomfort and even tissue damage.

#8: Your Body Responds to Your Mind More Quickly

Melanin exists in the brain, therefore, it is brain cells. When the same melanin cells found in your brain are present throughout your body, the message of movement can be passed much more quickly. This explains one of the reasons that blacks often excel in sports and dancing. It is because the message to move can be passed more quickly through the body, giving a better response time and improved ability.

SPIRITUAL BENEFITS OF MELANIN

#1: It Nourishes All the Cells of Your Being

One of the ways that melanin is charged is by being in the sun. When ultraviolet rays are reflected, the other light from the sun is absorbed through the skin. Here, this light energy becomes a nutrient that feeds all the cells of our body, giving them health and power. You can also create this nutrient by contact with radio waves, music, and cosmic waves. Your body absorbs, stores, and then distributes the melanin throughout the body, so all the cells can regenerate themselves. Some even say that you do not need to eat food and drink all the time to be healthy- deeply melanized individuals can charge from the sunlight.

#2: Melanin Lets You Emit Your Own Vibrational Frequency

Those with rich melanin stores have been discriminated against for many years, some people blaming distribution or wealth or being different. The truth is that those of African descent are looked at differently because they are different. As a melanated being, your source of creative energy is much greater than that of lesser melanated being. This spurs creative thought and when you have the attitude that you can accomplish, you can put forth the vibrational frequency that will determine what you receive from the world.

#3: You Can Learn to Be True to Yourself

Those who embrace melanin most effectively do so by aligning it with their values. They learn what they desire most and how they want to use this energy to create goodness in their lives. When you choose to acknowledge the power of melanin, you are reversing oppression. You learn to hold true to your values and then to work for the greater good in your life, regardless of if someone is willing to provide opportunity or not. When you embrace your melanin origins, you open the door to the universe and the physical world will no longer stand in your way.

#4: You Will Not Die with Regrets

You and you alone have the power to decide what to do with the knowledge that you will learn as you continue in this world. Melanin often gives those in tune with it great and powerful ideas. When you use these ideas, they become your reality. You will live at peace, instead of with the guilt that you never put your great ideas into motion. You will be remembered, rather than leaving the world with just thoughts of what you could have been.

#5: You Become Free

Finally, when you begin to embrace your melanin on a spiritual level, you begin to free yourself. Through centuries of history, the African population has been seen as the lesser species. They have been oppressed and taken advantage of simply because other racial groups were frightened of what would happen should the African race realize their true potential. When you do realize this potential, you become free. By realizing that you are deeply connected with the cosmos and that you do not have to be a victim to the oppression that surrounds you, you liberate yourself and liberate your soul.

These suppressed truths are just some of the knowledge that melanin is capable of, on a physical and spiritual level. As you read, think about how the different steps will bring these benefits into your life. Realize these benefits and put your plans into action.

CHAPTER 3: THE PRESENCE OF MELANIN ON A SPIRITUAL LEVEL

It is true that the physical presence of melanin in your being presents immediate benefits, such as protecting the tissues of your skin, eyes and cells. However, the melanin that exists within those of African descent on a spiritual level is much more advanced. It is this melanin of your spirit that has the potential to change your entire life.

The Direct Relationship Between Skin Pigmentation and Brain Cells

Before the embryo becomes a fetus, the outer layer of skin (the ectoderm) produces melanin. This melanin eventually helps grow into the brain, as it has 12 melanated centers which are known as black nuclei. The outer layer they grow in (the blastula) becomes the spinal cord and eventually the brain. The twelfth nuclei is considered the highest. This is the nuclei that will begin to form the brain, known as the locus coeruleus.

It is believed that the locus coeruleus is the closest human connection to spirituality and an altered state of consciousness. This is also the area of the mind that allows humans to access the dream world. It is believed that this dream world allows us to learn from our past ancestors, that we can channel the creative powers of those of African descent who have walked the earth. Though we are both part of the animal kingdom, animals typically have a lighter pigment than those of African descent. Less of them have pigmented 'centers' in their mind, thus, they will not all be able to reach the same level of consciousness that humans can.

The chlorophyll of plants also has a similarity to the spiritual melanin of a human. The melanin within you always seeks greatness and is only held back by the limitations that you put on it. Plants take in their melanin as sun also using it for food to promote growth. As a plant grows, it often grows toward the sunlight of the earth, finding the best, brightest food source and reaching toward it. As human beings, our melanin content can also motivate us to reach to higher developed states of consciousness, learning what our true values are and then using the power of melanin to manifest our desires in the world.

The Spiritual Beliefs of Early African Scientists

Before the time of oppression, African scientists realized the incredible connection between the melanin of their skin and the melanin of their mind. It was believed that the connection of carbon and black melanin life force, was divine, for it was within all things that inhabit the earth. Ancient Africans often called themselves various names that meant black, like 'Kemites', which means people of the black earth. Scientists of the time worked hard to uncover the secret inner workings of their mind, understanding the relationship between the mind and body. Eventually, these scientists learned that the level of 'blackness' of the skin was directly related to a higher level of spirituality and inner vision. Those who realized this connection realized the divine presence within them. They realized the vibratory energies that swirled around them, all the different shades of black that existed as the color of the ocean of outer space that is the universe. The dark matter is the birthplace of all the planets in the solar system, the stars in the sky, all the galaxies in the universe and all the living and non-living things that exist in the cosmos. The purest presence of this carbon, this black matter, is the black holes that are scattered across the universe. These black holes are the richest source of carbon in the universe, as all they do is absorb all energy that comes into their path.

The role of carbon in all this has to do with the chemical form of melanin. Melanin can be thought of as a chain of carbon atoms that have lined together. This incredible chemical captures light and has the potential to reproduce itself. Within the brain, black neuromelanin is the core of what is responsible for inner vision and intuition. It is also responsible for one's spiritual illumination and creative genius. The reason that melanin opens all these pathways is because it allows you access to the inner workings of the subconscious mind. Within the subconscious mind lies the wisdom of your ancestors, like a timeless memory bank that has collected all the information learned by the knowledgeable, creative Africans that have walked this earth and learned to harness their incredible spiritual energy.

One of many great scientists discussed was George Washington Carver. Carver is credited with discovering the many uses of the peanut, but there is more to his story. Some scholars believe that it was not his Master's Degree in Chemistry that allowed him to come up with all his original genius ideas, but the knowledge of self they drove his discoveries.. George Washington Carver was very dark in nature and had an incredible mind, one that was open and receptive to the creative genius of the black melanin of his brain. Carver was noted to take early morning strolls, which he believed fostered an environment to absorb sunlight and clear his conscious, which guided him to take the next step in his research. The problem with this theory was the effect that it had on African American children, who began to resist traditional teaching methods because they desired to be in tune with nature and preferred to learn outside.

Your Melanin Gives You the Power to Control Your Vibrational Frequency

Melanin has the power to absorb and to put forth. As you charge your melanin, you give it greater power. However, you should not confuse this great power with getting what you want. The vibrational frequency put forth from your melanin has the potential to be positive or negative. It is what you choose to consciously do with this power that will go out into the world. As you create this vibrational frequency, that which is similar will come to you in abundance.

Create a high vibrational frequency, refusing to let negative thoughts and excessive worry into your mind. When you emit this high frequency of melanin, it attracts other high frequencies. This is because whatever you choose to resonate as your own energy, you attract. This works similar to the way that glass breaks when a high note is sung.

Many people believe that breaking a glass with a high note is a parlor trick of sorts. However, there is a science behind the way that it works. Think for a moment of the sound that a glass makes when a small metal tine is struck against it to make a sound. Imagine this as a chord. When the note carried from the vocal chords of the singer reach the same frequency of the glass, it breaks. The energy in this scenario starts in the singer's vocal chords, traveling across as a sound. Then, the energy is pushed into the air of the throat before being pushed out through the mouth and into the surrounding area. This energy then moves through the air, being attracted to the glass. As it starts to equal the energy of the glass, the two sounds resonate as one. This creates a great vibration, one that moves through the glass. When the glass can contain no more energy, the vibration is strong enough that the glass breaks.

MELANIN AND RACE

When most people think of the first people on the earth, especially those who follow the Bible, they think of Adam and Eve. Though the skin color of these 'first people' has never been scientifically examined, it is commonly believed that they were white. However, if the first people were white, how could they create a melanated being? While people with lower levels of melanin can seek sunlight and attract more melanin, this will eventually fade with time. Even if it is maintained, a person with this low level of melanin could never become as dark as those of true African descent. It would make sense, therefore, that Africans were the first beings. As people with melanin deficiencies bore children that were lighter, other races were created from the African race. Migration to different areas, farther away from the equator, also played a role in the lighter skin tones that would contribute to future races. This is one of the things that makes those of African descent so incredible on a spiritual level. All races, those of brown, yellow, and white skin tones, are derived from this original African race. It is impossible to create someone of pure African descent from all the less-melanated races of the world, but it is possible to derive all the different melanin states from an African bloodline. In some people with a lighter complexion, there melanin appears as clusters of freckles on areas of the body that get the most natural sun exposure.

THE FOUR CATEGORIES OF RACE

Scientists who have studied how melanin relates to race from a cosmic perspective have classified humans into four groups according to the amount of melanin contained within their body and the spectrum of light that can be absorbed as a result. To understand this, remember that melanosomes are tiny pockets in which the potential (or lack of potential) of the body to create melanin lies.

Stage 1: Someone with Stage 1 melanin levels has empty melanosomes. They do not possess the necessary equipment to make melanin. These types of people maybe melanin recessive and may need to adjust their diet or increase sun exposure to remain healthy.

Stage 2: A person with Stage 2 melanin levels has the ability to make melanin. Their body has plenty of potential, but the melanosomes themselves are empty of melanin.

Stage 3: An individual with Stage 3 has access to some of their melanin, as they possess the machinery to create melanin and also have melanosomes that are filled half-way with melanin.

Stage 4: At this stage, the individual likely has a dark complexion. Their body possess the necessary machinery to make melanin and also has melanosomes that are completely filled with melanin.

People of Caucasian descent have Stages 1 and 2. While they all possess melanin to an extent, they do not necessarily possess the melanin levels necessary to connect on a spiritual level. It is common for people of Asian, Latino, and Hispanic descent to be Stage 3, with skin tones that are not light but that contain at least some degree of melanin. Those of

African descent are common to Stages 3 and 4, depending on the purity of the melanin within. Regardless, Stages 3 and 4 have the most potential for connecting to the universe on a cosmic level and bringing your great ideas and your deepest desires into existence in the physical world. People of color also have circulating melanin, which is caused when excess melanin spills from the melanosomes into the blood and circulates through the body. In a way, those like albino people who may be melanin recessive, may even be seen as having a genetic disorder.

RACIAL BACKGROUND AND ENERGY ABSORPTION

We see the color of those around us as we would everyday objects. The light is absorbed or reflected off of the individual's skin, depending on their melanin content. Skin color, therefore, is a matter of perception, but melanin content is not. The amount of melanin within your skin determines the range of light energy that can be absorbed. Those with Stage 4 melanin can absorb the entire light spectrum, from basic electric power to the great cosmic waves. Those with Stage 1 melanin can absorb a very limited amount of the light spectrum, which means they must intake their melanin from other sources. They also cannot absorb this wide range of energy that gives black people their profound abilities.

HYPER PERCEPTION

Melanin is highly integrated in the nervous system of African American human beings. This nervous system is what is responsible for perceiving the world around us. It is what gives us the ability to perceive what we see, smell, taste, feel and hear. We interpret these things and they become reality. Since those of African descent have such a connection between their mind and their skin, it is almost as if there is a second brain that grows on the outside of the body. It is this brain that perceives the world around you when you are of African descent, allowing you to be aware of all your surroundings. When you are in tune with this 'outer' brain, you become that much closer to the people and things around you. This means that as you experience life, you have a closer, more human experience because you can perceive all things.

MELANIN AND THE COSMOS: AN EXAMPLE

One highly studied group of Africans during ancient times is the Dogon Tribe of Mali. These African people have very deep melanin skin tones, so it would stand that they would be a Stage 4 level of melanin and have the ability to the entire universal energy spectrum.

The reason the Dogon people are so interesting is because they have explored the universe and uncovered and recorded intricate details of the cosmos beyond us, even before man went into space.

Some of the details they uncovered include where our star (the sun) lies, where the white dwarf companion of Sirius exists in the sky, the rings of Saturn, how the milky way has a spiral structure, and the moons of Jupiter. Even though you cannot see these things with the human eye, the Dogon tribe was able to observe and record them. The Dogons also uncovered them before the time of technological instruments. So, the question remains, how?

The Dogons relied on their existence as melanated beings. They were able to sense these astrological patterns, making record of them as drawing on their clothing and the huts that they lived in. This mystery plagued the Europeans in the years to come, especially since at the time this Dogon information was uncovered the Europeans had just started to uncover these cosmic entities- and that was only with the help of high-powered telescopes! The Dogons felt the existence of these cosmic entities, perceiving them with their second mind and recording this information as reality. This is something that would never be possible for someone who was melanin recessive.

Another example of this incredible power of melanin is the way that Ancient Africans communicated. There is a reason that Africans today are so incredible at the drum, especially tribes living within third-world countries. The drums are a means of communications. Ancient Africans could send these sounds and images using the drum, communicating with tribes who were hundreds of miles away from the source of the drumming.

If you compare the abilities of the Dogons and other African tribes of the time against the Europeans, it becomes clear that there is a major difference in their abilities to perceive the universe and use it for their understanding and advancement. This difference is not in the civilization or the access of materials, but in the ability of blacks to harness the ability of melanin on a cosmic level and use it for greatness.

African Hair, the Golden Spiral, and the Electricity of Melanin

The hair of those of African descent is also incredibly powerful, with its spirals and its ability to attract and store electricity giving those who wear it incredible potential.

THE GOLDEN SPIRAL

The spiral is something that can be seen through all of creation. The Golden Spiral is a symbol highly valued in the universe. It is said that all life is created of a spectrum of circles, each of these being weaved throughout one another. This spiral is found in birth and death, with every breath in and out, and in the differing worlds of day and night. It is often called the 'Divine Proportion', as this spiral and its constant can be found throughout the universe. It is present in the spirals of your fingertips and the shape of the human ear, as well as in the waves of the ocean, the double helix of the DNA molecule of all living things on the universe, the shape that roots and stems follow as they extend from seeds, seashells, and in all other things in the universe.

Every human being has these swirls on their heads, as even Caucasians have a whorl pattern from which hair sprouts on their head. However, those with straight hair have only this pattern, which comes to an end at the roots of their hair. As someone of African descent, your spirals extend beyond this initial whorl and into your hair. The longer your hair is, the more creative power you hold within it.

THE ELECTRICITY OF AFRICAN HAIR

When people think of 'African' hair, they often think of hair that is dark in color, wavy, thick, nappy and frizzy. This hair can be incredibly difficult to manage, as it seems to always be electrified and wanting to reach toward the skies. However, this is not necessarily a bad thing.

Have you ever appreciated your hair for what it truly was? It is not uncommon for men and women of African descent to wish they had more manageable hair, some of them even resorting to dying it, straightening it, and making it lie flat. When you make your hair lie flat, you are stopping your flow of power. When you dye your hair, you are taking away from its ability to absorb and attract all the electricity from the different spectrums of universal light. When you tamper with your true African hair, you are tampering with your ability to absorb and digest information from the sun.

Often, it is taught that true beauty is to have smooth, sleek, and beautiful hair. It is taught that lighter, fairer skin is beautiful. However, all is beautiful. This is a trick that diminishes what you truly are, by depleting your access to the great dark matter that covers the cosmos. Allow your hair to grow naturally. Style it, but do not use relaxers and other harmful ingredients that take away from the majestic being that you truly are. Learn to embrace your hair and value it for the incredible way that it pulls melanin and the creative power of the universe into your field so that you may shape it, project it, and bring the things that you desire into reality.

Chapter 4: Boosting Melanin Levels: What to Do and What to Avoid

It is true that we are born with melanin. This dark matter is our beginning and as someone of African descent, it is a gift to you in your life. It gives you the power of smooth, simple skin, the power of creative intelligence, and the power of directing energy so that you may choose what to attract in your life. However, when this black matter is neglected or avoided, it goes to waste. As you will read, you will learn the things that you should and should not do- to improve melanin levels and maximize your abilities and to prevent activities that deplete the melanin stores and the power you hold within.

WHAT YOU CAN DO: IMPROVE

TYROSINE LEVELS

Tyrosine has a profound effect on how much melanin is present in the body. In fact, tyrosine is known to cause albinism (white, colorless skin and sometimes red irises) when it is deficient. This means that when your body does not produce or you do not consume enough tyrosine, it depletes your stores of melanin and decreases your power. Even though tyrosine is an amino acid naturally produced by the body, sometimes the body's stores are not enough. There are three ways to boost tyrosine levels.

First, you can increase your intake of certain foods that have high concentrations of tyrosine. This includes seaweed, pumpkin flesh, mustard greens, cottage cheese, egg whites, tuna, kidney beans, sesame seeds, cod, avocado, spinach and bananas. Eating a variety of these types of food is sufficient for some people, especially those who regularly include these in their diet.

The second option is dietary powders or supplements. When you consume food sources of tyrosine, it will not all remain after the digestive process. Additionally, tyrosine is difficult to pass through the blood-brain barrier. When you choose to supplement with tyrosine, it is often in a form that is easily digested by the body. You also have the advantage of knowing how much tyrosine you are taking.

Finally, you can consume foods or supplement with phenylalanine. Phenylalanine is the precursor to tyrosine, meaning that the body makes tyrosine from phenylalanine. It is also absorbed much easier through the blood-brain barrier so it is more accessible to your body. You can supplement phenylalanine with a capsule or powder, or you can get it from your diet. Some good sources of this amino acid include fish (including crab, cod, catfish, tuna, sardines, lobster, oysters, and mussels), which has an entire day's requirement in a portion, meats including chicken, turkey, beef, and liver, gelatin, eggs, dairy products including cheese, milk, and cream cheese, nuts, legumes like lentils and chickpeas, soy products and aspartame.

WHAT YOU CAN DO: RECHARGING YOUR MELANIN IN YOUR DAILY LIFE

In addition to taking in melanin using dietary means, it is important that you recharge your melanin naturally as well. Doing things like being out in the sun, early morning walks, or moving through dance are just some of the ways that you can recharge your solar power. It is also important to get enough sleep. It is shown that the pineal gland is most active between the hours of 11 p.m. and 7 a.m., though it is only active while the mind is asleep. Get as much sleep as you can during this time to encourage the natural production of melanin. Sleeping during this time is also said to be the most enlightening, since it is the pineal gland that can open the mind to the world of the unconsciousness and even encourage lucid dreaming.

Sun exposure is highly recommended, to help you boost melanin and absorb the creative energies of the universe. Seek sunlight as often as you can. This will boost your immune system, as well as improve emotional and mental health. It is recommended that melanated individuals get at least 30 minutes of direct sunlight at least three times each week.

PRESERVING MELANIN: WHAT NOT TO DO

Just as you must encourage melanin production in your body, there are certain things that should be avoided to ensure your pineal gland and melanin are at their fullest capabilities. Here is what you need to know:

• <u>Avoid fluoridated water- Most cities treat their water with fluoride, even though it has been proven to have some adverse health effects. One of these effects is calcification of the pineal gland, which minimizes its capability and power. Avoid city water to prevent</u>

this calcification. Do not worry if you have been drinking or cooking with fluoridated water- just stop immediately. You can decalcify it to re-open the pineal gland by using detoxifiers like ginseng, Bentonite clay, chlorophyll, and blue-green algae or by consuming detoxifying foods like seaweed, cilantro, bananas, coconut oil, honey, and watermelon.

• Do not take Vitamin-D supplements- Vitamin D supplements can be dangerous for melanated individuals, especially if you follow the recommended guidelines for getting enough sun each week. Do this naturally instead of supplementing, as the body naturally produces Vitamin D from exposure to the sun. If you are melanin recessive, you may need to supplement but it is still recommended that cod liver oil be used rather than Vitamin D. Vitamin D is hard to absorb, while cod liver oil is easier to absorb and promotes the natural production of Vitamin D by the body.

• Avoid fatty foods- Melanin bonds with fatty compounds, which has two effects. First, it can make you gain weight more easily than someone with less melanin would. Second, it traps your melanin and lessens your ability to harness its power. For this reason, avoid animal fats, saturated fats, and vegetable oils. Instead of choosing vegetable oils, consider those rich in Omega-3s like coconut oil, olive oil, or grapeseed oil.

Chapter 5: Your Responsibility to Harness Your Abilities from Melanin

Stop for a moment think of how you are living your life. How are people going to remember you when you are dead and gone? Will anyone but your family know your name? Will you have made an impact on the people of the world? As an intelligent being, you have a responsibility to ensure that you when you are lying on your deathbed, people are remembering your legacy. By reading this book and learning of the incredible life you are blessed to experience, you place yourself in the footsteps of your ancestors. This debt is the debt of doing what you can to lie the foundation for the future- to be a part of the great change that will occur in the world when knowledge of self is restored.

YOUR RESPONSIBILITY: WHAT YOU OWE THE WORLD

There is not any single physical thing or gift that you can give the world for it to suffice as your mark on the world. That which you owe the world is not a physical thing, but the use of your free will. Your responsibility is to use your knowledge for the greater good. We are creatures of light, love and peace.

When you die, there are two possible scenarios. In the first, you are remembered by all those that love you. They are not sad merely because your physical body is passing on, but because they remember all that you have done in life. They are remembering how you have used your own intellectual wealth and the power that comes along with it to help those that you could. They are remembering all the great ideas that have flowed forth from your mind and all the memorable words that you have given. They are remembering how great you are and how all the world will be at a loss once you have breathed your last breath.

The second scenario is a sad one. You may still be surrounded with those that love you, but you will not see them. Instead, you are going to see all the ideas that you had surrounding you. You are going to see all the things that you wish you had said and wish you had done to leave an impact on the world. In this scenario, your room is full of all the ifs of your life. It is full of all the things that could have been. It is full of those kids who may have tried harder, had you shared your story or those people who were not helped by the incredible ideas that you kept into your head, because you always thought there would be more time.

There is no single place on earth that is wealthier than the graveyard. The graveyard is filled with the unlimited potential of all the people who have been laid to rest without leaving their mark on the world. It is filled with the unrealized dreams of all that lie there, of the speeches that were never given and the inventions that were never created because the person lying in that graveyard believed they had more time.

Your responsibility to the world is to stop holding back. Stop letting races that believe they are greater than you tell you that you are not enough. Stop letting people tell you that you cannot go further or you cannot embrace your dreams, because you are not good enough or smart enough or strong enough. Refuse to accept the lie pushed onto those of the African race; the lie that you must wait for others to open doors for you before you can realize your dreams. You are enough and you will be enough, regardless of what others think or say. The power of melanin has been hidden for a long time, but it is time for it to be realized. It is time for people rich in this black, creative matter of the universe to step forth and start making the changes that are necessary in the world.

Stop Now and Realize This

The few paragraphs that follow are among the most important in this book. Read these and know that they are the truth. Read these and feel the power flow through you. Feel the melanin express in your being and experience it as you never have before. Think of all your ideas and your thoughts that you may have wanted to imprint on the world but didn't, because you did not think anyone would listen or because you thought that it was not your place. Perhaps you lacked the motivation and energy. Realize the following words and know that you do have the power to change the world, as soon as you start to take advantage of the benefits embedded in your mind.

People of African descent have the power of melanin in every single cellular structure that exists in our being. It makes up our bodies and it flows through our blood. Melanin is condensed sunlight, full of intelligent information. By refusing to realize and use this gift, we allow the world around us to put us under their oppression. The oppression we face in our lives comes from external sources, but we have the power of deciding if we want to accept it. When you let the negative energy around you shape who you are, it acts as an oppressive force and you respond by limiting yourself. Instead of creating yourself out of the creative intelligence and brilliance that lives within your melanated mind, you create yourself in their oppressive image. In this way, you defeat yourself.

Make the decision to stop this oppression. Make the decision to create your own energy frequency. Do not create energies based on what you are told you may have, but rather what you want. Create your own frequency and then create your own energy. Project the positive mindset and become who you were meant to be from that moment of conception in your life. It is when you make this decision, the decision to become who you were meant to be and to start imparting your unique energy and your love in the world around you, that you can change the world. You must use your intellectual wisdom to do great things, using this wisdom and your creativity in conjunction with the power of free will, you can reach that higher frequency.

To operate on this higher frequency, you must shut out the world and become who you are within. Refuse to live in menial environments and accept less than what you deserve. Raise your expectations and raise your frequency and watch as the universe comes to your beckoning. Watch as the universe responds to this higher frequency and responds to your desires, changing the world around you. Do this for yourself and then do this for your people, demanding what you deserve from life and make change.

As you do this, remember. It is a lie that you are inferior. It is a lie that you must wait around to be handed things and that you must wait for doors to be opened for you. Know that the melanin that flows through your blood and fills every cell of your body is chemical evidence of your greatness. Acknowledge its presence, and embrace. Take complete advantage of it and know that with your conscious, you can create the reality of your world.

UNDERSTANDING AND OVERCOMING

RACISM

It has been proven time and time again that as children, we are born without hate. Children and animals in infancy, from that first breath on the planet, hate no one and no thing. Racism, therefore, is a learned thing. Or is it? Why is it that so many people are willing to hate?

While racism is learned, it is also something that has been ingrained in history. As humans have evolved, so have our brains. Even so, there is an ancient part of the brain, the oldest part that exists, that is designed specifically for survival. It is this part of the brain that is required to detect anything that is potentially dangerous or that seems off. When detected, the mind creates a fight-or-flight reaction by pumping hormones like adrenaline and cortisol through the body. While the mind has evolved, this part of the brain exists. It hides, lurking in the depths, but still sometimes affecting what goes on in the subconscious mind. It is by understanding this ancient part of the brain that you can begin to understand the racism that exists in the world and why.

Do you remember the Dogon Tribe of Mali and the Europeans that existed not long after? Do you remember how much more advanced the Dogons were, knowing of things that the Egyptians had only just started to explore? This incredible knowledge that was so advanced for their time period that it could only be inferred that they were superior. Unfortunately, instead of seeking to learn from the intellectual power and creative prowess of the blacks, other societies tried to oppress it. They were not impressed by it, but terrified, terrified of what melanated beings could do if they chose to stand together as one.

The outward hostility that whites show toward blacks goes beyond that of a fear of losing wealth. It is theorized that whites may act this way because of their wealth and their interest in protecting their own wealth, but this is not the case. This racism has been deeply ingrained in the most ancient part of the mind out of fear. Early people knew that blacks were the creator of the other races, that it was the pigment, the melanin that gave them their power. They knew that our genetic makeup was different and that it was dominant, that it was our pigment that would shine through should we make children with someone of a lighter pigment. Once it was uncovered that the existence of melanin was greater in those of African descent and that melanin plays both biological and cosmic roles in the universe, it is no surprise that this greatness was oppressed. It is this melanin, not because of our skin color, but because of our minds, that is the greatest secret.

FIGHT-OR-FLIGHT AND AFRICANISM

If you look back at African history, there are many occurrences in many different countries of African slavery. Slavery is not a new idea. Even in the times of the Bible there were slaves, with one of the earliest occurrences being the Israelites held in Egypt. This is because, it has been known the melanated being possess great influence over the world, and is deeply connected to the cosmos. It was a basic fight-or-flight reaction; oppression as a means of fighting against what was perceived as a potential threat.

People who argue against this oppression may point to celebrities or politicians that are African, but these are just small examples. The elite societies do not fear people of color rising to positions of power or being given opportunities, because they still are not united as a whole, in addition our history is scattered about the Earth. The true root of the fear is that melanated beings will discover their true selves. In the times of White supremacy, blacks were robbed of their identity. They were dictated as to what they should do, how it should be done and even who they should be as a person. By accepting this as our history and by continuing to remain ignorant of our origins, we continue to be subservient to a supremacist idea. Even though we are past the time of slavery, blacks are still enslaved because they adhere to the labels and guidelines that have been forced upon them by society. In other words, defeat the system, by rising above the system. Empower your mind, and spread knowledge and love throughout the universe

These guidelines were put into place for a reason- Make no mistake your true identity has been hidden. However, the second that we begin to understand ourselves, our relation to the universe, the creative and intellectual power that exists within us, we begin to heighten our conscious. People will emit negative energy regardless. They may tell you to limit yourself, or be reserved in your actions. Do not stop. Refuse to let your creations go un-invented and refuse to let your words go unheard. Create and speak. Remember that you are incredible.

THE INCREDULITY OF YOUR BEING

The first step in realizing our incredulity, of realizing the potential that we have, is realizing how unique we truly are. Consider the structure of your cellular body. Did you know that every second you are alive, your body replaces 10 million of these melanin-rich cells, with stronger, healthier replacements for the old cells? Within three months, every single cell that makes up your current structural being will be gone but you will still exist. This is because you are made of a supreme intelligent design. Even with evolution and your ever-changing body, you remain uniquely you. Your form is not randomly acquired, therefore, your existence is not a mere mistake. It happened for a reason and by refusing to seek to learn that reason and refusing to learn what impact it is you can make on the world, you are cheating yourself and all those who sacrificed before you, who walk beside you, and who will walk after you. There is no thing or creation or event in this world that is accidental. There is not a single thing that happens just because. Cause and effect is always at play. The moment you realize this, you will stop becoming the effect and you will start creating the cause. As you do this, you become the cause in your life and what you reap as a result becomes the effects. Step into the role of your design and begin to act as a person fulfilling that design should act.

The evidence of your greatness is all around you. Look around at the people who have adapted your culture. Look at the music, food, inventions and culture that were wholly African but that have been adopted by other cultures, without the slightest acknowledgement. Know this occurs because they are attracted to your frequency. Know that this is your greatness and continue to strive. Strive first as an individual and then as a group, using your thoughts and creations and those thoughts and creations of other spiritual beings to assure your rightful place in the world at last.

The final thing that you must remember, as you go onto become all that you are capable of, is that even with higher knowledge comes responsibility. Do not try to take from or oppress others on your quest to greatness. Know that as you interact, we are all different but important. No person is superior, but we should all have our rights to succeed and excel in this world. Simply refuse to accept any label that is pushed upon you. Do not accept the mediocracy or the 'just living' that is afforded to you. Instead, use the vibrational energy that has been gifted to you since the moment of your creation to branch out and create your own reality.

CHAPTER 6: TECHNIQUES YOU CAN USE TO HARNESS THE ENERGY OF MELANIN

Up to this point, you have learned what melanin is, what it can do, how to use its energy responsibly, and how to best maintain the melanin levels in your body—but how do you use it? This chapter will teach you exactly what you need to know to start using all this energy that has been absorbed in the melanosomes of your body.

Step 1: Foster a Positive Mindset

Positivity is the first essential element of using the melanin in our lives. Do not mistake melanin for this great force that will create great things in your life regardless of what you put into it. Melanin does create, but it can create both positive and negative. For this reason, start each day with a positive mindset.

The first thing that you should do is called priming. Priming is an exercise that helps you reach an optimal state in your mind, one that is prepared to send out positive vibrational energies. This is important because if you let negative thoughts creep into your mind and bring you down, you bring your vibrational frequencies down. This can attract undesirable or even unpleasant things from the world around you, since the energy you emit creates your reality. If you act and think as if you are helpless, what the universe will deliver you is helplessness. The way to overcome this is to focus on your creative and positive energies, feeling confident that you can create the solution to any problem you may come across. Always start the day by clearing your mind of any negative thoughts. Avoid complaining, verbally acknowledge the good. If you do hear negative thoughts, release them from your mind. Assure yourself that a solution is available and return to the positive.

The second thing you should do is create a mindset of gratitude. Be thankful for what you do have. The reason that this is so important is because without an attitude of gratefulness for what you already have, you cannot be happy. Without happiness, you cannot possibly have a positive mindset. Create a list of at least 5 things that you are grateful for and take a moment to relish in them, being appreciative that you have each in your life.

Step 2: Block Out Negativity

It is true you cannot always control the world around you. You cannot control that your company is laying people off or that you were cut off in traffic. What you can control, however, is how you react to these things. Negative thoughts are sure to creep into your mind as you go about your day, especially if you get bad news or find yourself faced with an obstacle. In these times, you must block out the negativity and remember that the solution is available. Trust in your instincts and that creative power that resides in yourself. Push any negative thoughts you may be having from your mind. As you do, affirm that you will be okay. Affirm that regardless of what the future holds, you will find the solution that once again propels you to the top. Embrace the Yin and Yang.

Step 3: Envisioning Your Desires

When you imagine something, you bring it that much closer into being. Over the last decade, many studies have been done that researched the pathways of the brain and how they light up during certain activities. Several studies have found that imagining something in full detail lights up the same pathways that would be created if you were actually having that experience. The mind cannot tell whether it is creating a scenario or living it. This brings you closer to your desires, as your mind guides you to think and act in a way that attracts that scenario to your life.

As you envision what it is you want, choose an area where you can completely focus. Think of the scenario with as much detail as you can, from the way that your date's perfume/cologne smells to the way you will shake your client's hand before the presentation. Think of each detail and then re-play this scenario again and again until it becomes the truth in your life.

Step 4: Listen to the Melanin Within

You cannot expect that which you want most to happen overnight, nor without you putting in the work. Continue to create a positive attitude and learn to listen to the flow of your melanin. When you have a creative thought, embrace it, instead of pushing it away. When you have a great idea and your conscious mind pushes you to be quiet, because you think you will be shunned, speak it anyway. Learn to go with the flow of your life and remain open to what your life force may be guiding you to do. It is in this way that you will realize what you can do to help promote your own life and the lives of others.

Step 5: Remember to Recharge Your Melanin

As you embrace higher self, and give conscious to your energy, you must remember to recharge it. Otherwise, you will find that your motivation dwindles away. You may also find that you feel weaker and even experience illness more often. Go out in the sun often and seek out other forms of light to absorb. Dance to music, create your own rhythm, and remember to get a full night of sleep. Do all those things that your body needs so that as you realize the things you want in your life, you remain healthy enough and strong enough to seek them.

CONCLUSION

Through our lives, we are often taught that to succeed, we must work twice as hard. We are taught that we are supposed to live a certain lifestyle and become a certain person. By accepting this as our realities, however, we are cheating ourselves and all the generations to come.

As melanated beings, we are powerful. Every core of our being is made up of melanin, the dark matter that exists in every living and nonliving being of the universe. We must learn to embrace this energy and to focus our will that thrives within us to create our own vibrational energies in the universe. Through the creation of these energies, we can realize greatness and bring the things that we deserve to be.

Stop allowing outside forces to oppress you. Learn to embrace your melanated nature. Do not be ashamed of your natural skin or hair and realize it for the beauty, for the power, for the magnificence that it truly is. Learn to accept this as your truth and live as the designer of your reality.

Always seek to multiply your melanin so that your melanosomes are filled as much as they may be. Seek out the sun so you may tan and listen to the right music. Find the energy sources that you thrive on and seek them as often as possible. Use this to broadcast your own frequency and bring what it is that you want into being. Understand your nature and the truth of your being and allow this to bring what it is that you desire most in the world. Resist all the negative imprints of the world around you and understand that you operate at a level intimidating to others. Use this knowledge not to seek control or to destroy others, but to create a reality unlike one that you have ever imagined. Remember that you are light, love and peace. All you have to do to remember who you are, is simply stand in the sun.

As you embark on your journey of self-discovery, remember to use your energy in a way that would pride your ancestors and in a way that will benefit future generations. Never accept false pretenses- raise your standards and strive to spread your ideas and your messages until it becomes the truth of the world.

You and you alone have the power to create your own reality.

THE POWER OF AN EMPATH & NATURAL HEALER FOR BEGINNERS

SECTION 1: WHAT IS AN EMPATH?

Let's talk about the definition of the word empath. The meaning of empath is a person with the ability to apprehend, take on, and reflect the mental or emotional state of an individual. It also includes the ability to heal. An empath can also be described as someone who feels the feelings of others and takes on the emotions and feelings of those around them, a highly *sensitive* person. You may also have the feeling of "knowing" and "intuition". Sensing events before they happen and a strong and certain gut feeling when something doesn't feel right. Empaths have an extremely reactive neurological system and do not possess the same filters that other people do to block out stimulation. Some call it a blessing, some call it a curse.

Below you will find a list of questions to ask yourself, and if your answer is yes to many or all of the questions, you are indeed an empath.

- Do you find it hard to be around large groups of people?

- Do you sense things before they happen?

- Are you able to identify when someone is lying?

- Are you affected by the actions of others on a very emotional level?

- Do you have frequent stomach aches and migraines?

- When you are around cell phones, computers, etc do they malfunction?

- Do you feel waves of energy be it positive or negative when you walk into a room?

- Are you often exhausted after a simple trip to the grocery store?

- Is it hard and almost unbearable for you to watch violence of any kind? (Movies, real life, etc)

- Do you avoid or find it difficult to watch the news and sad media images?

- Do you take on the personalities of those around you?

- Are you often the receptacle for other people's problems, fears, and insecurities?

- Do smells and sounds have an affect on you?

- Are you someone that needs a lot of alone time to refresh and recharge?

- Do you often see yourself repulsed by selfish people and narcissists?

- Do you find a need for the truth and cannot stand even a hint of inauthenticity?

- Do you have frequent mood swings?

- Do you have very realistic and intense dreams?

- Do you sense prior events, past actions, or emotions when you walk into a room or walk past a building or area?

If you answered yes to most and or all of these questions then you are an empath and you are now on a journey to enlightenment and self discovery. For many, they experience this beginning in their childhood having no idea why they were feeling the emotions they experienced. For others it may be later in life. It can be overwhelming and difficult to understand what is happening and to embrace the awakening and change beginning within you but there are for sure benefits to realizing who you are and why you feel the things that you feel.

Empaths are natural healers and easy to befriend in a world full of sharks and monsters. This world can be an ugly place and healers such as empaths bring a comfort and light into a dark place. Do you find yourself very good at massages and natural ability to heal someone or make them feel better? Be it by listening to them or laying hands on them. Both are possible as an empath. You feel everything emotionally and with that ability you can see through pain and the layers of denial on top and get to the source to fix or "heal" the problem.

There are different types of empaths. Let's name and discuss the significance of each one.

- **Emotional Empaths** pick up other people's emotions and can become a sponge for the feelings

- **Physical Empaths** - are truly in step with other people's emotions and physical state. Also has the ability to absorb them into their body.

- **Intuitive Empaths** experience extraordinary perceptions such as heightened intuition, messages in dreams, telepathy, animal & plant communication, as well as contact with the other side.

There are several types of *Intuitive Empaths*:

- **Earth Empaths** > are in tune with the changes in the weather, planet, and solar system.

- **Telepathic Empaths** > receive intuitive information about others in the present time.

- **Dream Empaths** > have vivid dreams and receive information from those dreams that provide guidance to those around them, those that may not know, and to their own lives.

- **Animal Empaths** > are able to understand, tune in, and communicate with animals

- **Plant Empaths** > can feel the need of plants and connect with them

- **Precognitive Empaths** > have precognitive visions of the future whether dreaming or awake

- **Mediumship Empaths** > can access beings on the other side

Granted there are many people in the world who do not believe in these sorts of things, such as power, energy, or even magic. But in order to go forward, in order to truly understand who you are, you must believe. If you're a person that laughs these sort of beliefs off, then you will not be able to embrace and strengthen your abilities. You will be confused by the mood swings and emotions. You will stay in a sense of blindness and darkness never fully understanding or reaching your true potential.

When it comes to discussing those who may not believe in these sorts of things, it is very easy to find these types of people all around you in turn making it difficult to find someone to share your emotions and concerns with on this subject. Believe me, some of the things you experience as an empath isn't something you can broadcast on an everyday basis to certain people. They may think you need help, laugh at you, call you sensitive or dramatic, or maybe think you need to be locked away. When presenting information I've learned it helps to be incredibly honest and for empaths and those alike, this can be the unfortunate reality if you do not learn more and learn what and who to keep in your personal space. When you deal with limited and negative minds, and people that do not believe you or understand what you go through, it can cause you to suppress your gifts and even make you feel as if you are actually crazy or just hearing things when it is indeed much more happening within.

Empaths truly care about others feelings but resent lying and pretending of any kind. Phony behavior tends to turn an empath completely off. They tend to be very honest and can be a tad rough with the truth but that is only because any hint of fakeness or being around an inauthentic personality really will bother their soul and inner self. They tell it like it is very often. Now of course everyone has told a lie or weren't completely honest about a situation, be it in childhood or as an adult but empaths can see through it usually based completely off the energy the person they are speaking to gives off, body language and a strong sense of intuition.

"I've learned that people will forget what you said, people will forget what you did, but people will never forget how you made them feel" - Maya Angelou

A wonderful quote that often crosses my mind. This is exceptionally true. That is why people say another often quoted line "first impressions are everything". Because after meeting someone, you normally remember and feel more about how they made you feel and less about what they were wearing or doing. Feelings are everything and so is emotion. They are what drives humanities behavior. We as empaths feel these emotions very very strongly. We have a heightened sense and feeling of how someone made us feel and based on that, we then are able to determine if we want to be around them or not. For empaths it is literally for the sake of their health and mental stability that are careful who they are around.

THE DIFFERENCE BETWEEN AN

EMPATH AND EMPATHY

The definition of empathy is the ability to understand and share the feelings of others. I can understand the similarity with the word "empathy" and its meaning but there are distinct differences between it and the word "empath". Anyone can have empathy even though not everyone does. Anyone can "sympathize" with a situation without having any emotional attachment to it. They'll mouth the words of comfort and may seem as if they genuinely want to help but it does not go beyond it. There are others who feel absolutely nothing when told of a shocking event and they seem to not feel anything. Everyone is different.

Anyone can "understand" that someone may be going through a tough situation and metaphorically may place themselves in their shoes but only to that extent. So we've established that empathy is something anyone can feel and exhibit but being an empath is something more in depth and the two are often confused with one another.

An empath not only understands what someone is going through but becomes emotionally invested in the person's problems, feelings, and emotions. As stated above, an empath has the ability to apprehend feelings and literally take on what another person is feeling. Meaning they actually have the capacity to feel sick if someone around them is, or feel sad if someone around them is. Genuine feelings, not just feeling the same energy someone else is feeling because they're in the same room. It is much more than that. Empaths also have the ability to manipulate emotions to their benefit and or to the benefit of others. That may sound bad but it is not. Being an empath comes with the advantage of being able to turn negative energy regardless of the size, into something positive. To be able to literally absorb negative energy from a person and they'll end up leaving the area or conversation feeling much lighter leaving the empath completely drained but now needing to release or purify all the negative energy they absorbed.

There is absolutely nothing wrong with empathy but sometimes more is needed than someone's pity and sympathy. Sometimes more is needed than their understanding. Empathetic people are compassionate people and there is always a need for understanding what someone is going through but empaths can literally heal when fully aware of their powers. They have a listening ear unlike any other. They can pierce into the heart and feel the energy of a person.

GROWING UP AS AN EMPATH

Empathic abilities can begin in childhood. Have you experienced deep emotions and energy as a kid? Were you very sensitive to sound and violence on games or movies at a young age? It is very possible for empath abilities to start while very young. You can receive visions and feel emotions very intensely but no proper way to express that considering how young you may have been and how confusing all the feelings must be for someone so young.

Mine began around 9 years old and intensified as I got older. The more I could not express myself, the harder it was to understand what was happening. I started having intense visions of the near future even my own right around me when I was about 14 years old. But even younger than that I used to walk in crowds and feel so emotion and energy from people. I knew intently when a place or a person wasn't right without ever meeting them or going to that location.

The strong sense of intuition and sense of energy tells you so much growing up and if you learn to listen to it and develop it, it can help you through so many unknown paths in life. Growing up as an empath, simple experiences for others are draining and difficult for us. School may be especially difficult. All those kids, teachers, people, close hallways and constant interaction can be truly overwhelming. Not that it's too loud per say, though it may be for some, but there is a lot of emotion involved. On top of the homework and responsibilities, it can be a lot to handle.

Many parents don't know that their child may have this ability. They may assume that he or she is being dramatic or overly sensitive. When indeed it may actually be more. It can be confusing especially in the teenage years for sure, because you are turning into an adult, still learning yourself, and experiencing things that seem to be impossible. Most people don't believe in having visions, intuition, or the ability to actually "feel" energy so it can be difficult to tell or share this with anyone regardless of age but please understand that that is indeed what it is. It is what many consider "impossible".

WHAT IS ENERGY?

Energy is what we all are. Every human, every plant, every drink of water, every animal is all energy. The definition of energy is *"the strength and vitality required for sustained physical or mental activity."* The law of conservation of energy states that energy can be converted in form, but not created or destroyed. We are all life forms that are energy thus that is how we survive. Energy is like a strong force field to an empath. We feel "unseen" energy clear as day. Emotion is "Energy In Motion" and we feel every bit of it. Energy is found in everything. Humans, plants, animals, crystals, stones, rocks, the moon and sun.

THE CHAKRA

What is the Chakra and how does it coincide with the topic of energy? Well your chakras are said to be the energy centers in your body in which energy flows. The chakra is like a powerhouse of energy that is charged and recharged through contact with other high energy sources. Such as crystals, grounding stones and people. Chakras connect your spiritual body to your physical body. At times, chakras can become blocked due to stress, emotional problems, or physical issues. Though there are 7 known and often discussed chakras, there are actually 114. The human body contains thousands of energy channels and is an amazing and complex form of energy. Seven key chakras are the circular vortexes of energy and are placed in seven different points along the spinal column. Each chakra is connected to different organs and glands within the body.

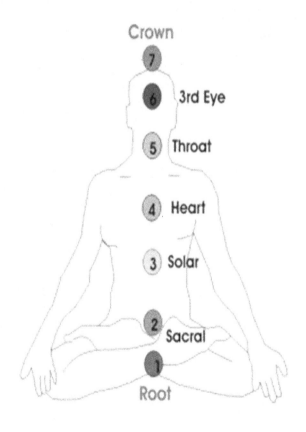

Emotion and what we experience as empaths and these energy sources or channels known as chakras coincide to a great degree. You want to keep these main channels clear because they can affect daily life. Let's take for example the heart chakra located in the middle of the chest. According to HIndu and Buddhists traditions, it is the fourth primary chakra. The heart chakra is associated with emotions, balance, calmness, and serenity. It in itself represents love. But coming in constant contact with negative energy can create blocks in your chakra and create feelings of sadness, depression and/or anger. Having protection such as crystals can help reduce the amount of bad energy that you may find yourself surrounded by as we will discuss further in this book. But for now, you can draw the connection between empaths, chakras and energy.

SECTION 2: EMPATHS AND EVERYDAY LIFE

Living in this loud and emotional world can cause major overwhelming feelings for an empath. Going to work can be complicated. Going to college and extracurricular activities can be exhausting. Even going to the grocery store and sitting in traffic can be too much. Every person you pass or interact with has the potential to pass their energy to you be it negative or positive. Considering how many people everyone can possibly see everyday, this can be a bit much on the body and mind.

You can't avoid the outside world altogether but you can learn how to embrace and develop the gifts you have to survive and be happy in it. That can be challenging at first.

Family gatherings are so much fun and people love going to functions with family and friends but as an empath you might be that one person that declines to go to every one of these events because of how they may make you feel. Outings are fun yes of course, but an empath is the one that can point out the fake one in the room immediately and even if everyone doesn't see it they will treat that person accordingly. An empath can feel when someone with negative energy and intentions is there no matter how hard they try and mask their behavior and words and can come off as mean, too honest, or distant from everyone at the gathering.

People may think your anti-social or just shy but in reality, the real question you're presented with in this situation is "how are you supposed to explain this to someone in these kinds of moments"? That you can feel more than what meets the eye. I can completely relate and to put a stop to this kind of situation, I simply just stopped going where I felt uncomfortable. I became completely indifferent if it was family or not. If I sense a hint of someone's ill intentions or thoughts towards me, manipulation, or their insecurities and/or jealousies are pushed onto me even indirectly, I stay completely from the area than to deal with the fake persona of being nice just to save face. Saving mental health and happiness should mean way more than saving face.

For anyone out there thinking that you are alone in feeling this way, you are not. There are indeed others alike who are searching for answers as well. I wanted to write this book from a down to earth and beginners point of you as I completely know what it's like to experience life as an empath and wonder who or what I could turn to. We can't avoid the public eye, everyone has to work or go out into the world at some point and yes it's taxing. Being around people in general can be taxing no matter who you are but for an empath this is especially so.

Relationships can also be particularly difficult in an empath's everyday life. Friendships, marriages, coworkers and parenting can be tough and the simplest events and times may seem overwhelming emotionally but you can overcome this. Being in a solid relationship is good and recommended for an empath. You need someone there to share your thoughts with and someone to help you grow in this world as everyone does, but because empaths are also very generous, caring, and sometimes naive people they can fall into very toxic relationships and friendships.

The giving and healing nature of an empath can easily be taken advantage of in a world where most people only care about themselves. So when you come across an actual person that is loving and open and let's almost everything slide, people tend to take it a bit too far. You, the empath have to learn to guard against being drained and used to the extent where there is no part of you left. Do not give so much yourself away just because you feel sorry for people very easily. This goes with anyone that may be in your life at work or at home. Establish boundaries because relationships of any kind for us can be taxing on the mind as well as the body.

Relationships can also be tricky due to the amount of feelings and emotions we feel and it can be projected onto those we love making it hard sometimes to sustain relationships. Honesty helps when dealing with things such as these. Let your partner know the feelings you have and how they make you feel. Research the things you experience, you feel, the things you are around so that you not only have a better understanding about yourself but also find others that experience that same things you do, assuring you that you are not alone. Having support and being able to share your thoughts with like minded people is very strengthening.

It can be tricky to maintain a solid relationship when filled with not only your own emotions but also that of your spouse, significant other, and or friend. When you are around the person, you absorb their emotions as well, so to what may seem like an ordinary conversation to them, depending on the topic, may be too much for you mentally and may start to show physically. For example, someone is sharing with you why they came home upset, except instead of just hearing the story, the empath can now feel the emotion behind more than the words. If it's negative emotion you may feel sweaty, nervous, and a bunch of butterflies in your stomach. You may also feel yourself getting upset when you were feeling just fine.

Take care to understand and not to confuse the feelings of yourself and that of the person you are talking to. You are absorbing their energy. We will discuss further things you can do to and crystals you can keep with you for protection to help you fight against these feelings in everyday life and conversation. They are also tremendously helpful in stressful and traumatic situations.

WAYS TO PROTECT AND CONTROL YOUR EMOTIONS

As we established, emotions are a great portion of what you have to cope with as an empath. Empaths are more subject to the energies of other people. Their problems, their desires, their issues, their toxic negativity, and all the emotions and possibly physical pain that a person may be experiencing. So for an empath, having grounding stones and or crystals is especially critical. They aid in shielding your mind, guarding your emotions, and helps empaths feel more secure and have more confidence. There are crystals that also help hone and enhance intuition and psychic ability.

Let us first talk about crystals, their use, the different types, and their importance. Crystals are solid substances made from several different conditions in the earth and can form many different shapes all consisting of massive amounts of energy. The earth provides so much that is for our benefit and growth. It provides what we need. From the plants, trees, water, and oils, minerals, crystals, etc. Crystals are said to be the most stable form of matter in the universe.

A crystals grows within the earth's crust. The depth of the earth's crust contains high pressures of heat. Within each step of a crystals formation is energy. Crystallization then happens when the layers of the planets mantle fracture, then causing gases, heat, and liquids forced by high pressure, to flow to the surface.

In addition to the heat and liquid you have magnesium, water, oxygen, iron, sodium all present and in the process they all merge and dissolve with other elements all while being pushed to the surface. This mixture will continue to rise and pass through several layers of less active and cooler rock therefore forming crystals in the cavities rocks.

The environment is especially important in order for crystals to form. The correct mixture of the elements is crucial as mentioned above. The need of energy. The temperature, light and water are all key factors in a crystalized formation. The color, size and shape are all a result of this process. Like any other creature on earth, crystals are alive and full of earth's energy compatible with us as humans as we are also energy.

Crystals work with the human energy field with the ability to diffuse, shift and or absorb energy. Some have magnetic powers, many of them have extreme energy and power contained inside so that when held or touched by a person or even in the close proximity of a person or animal, that energy can be absorbed from the crystal.

The stones, crystals, and minerals of the earth are compatible with human energy and have been used for centuries in the spiritual world.

Crystals have profound healing effects. Healing crystals harness the life giving elements of the Earth and of the universe. A crystal harnesses energy from the Sun, the ocean, and the moon. Though they may have these powers and effects it takes practice and belief to open your mind and heart to allow the healing effects to take place.

Your intention and your the state of your mind are extremely vital in the use of crystals. Because remember, this is not a movie where if you just pick up a crystal it'll start glowing and you become all powerful. No it doesn't quite work like that. You must be grounded and connected to the earth and universe. You must also cleanse your mind and have healthy positive intentions so that the crystal connects with your mind and guide you in the right direction. Every person has a certain energy. Each one is different. Crystals pick up on everyone's unique vibrations and amplify the positive thoughts, feelings, and vibes that they're cultivating. Albert Einstein said that everything in life is a vibration and just like "sound waves" your thoughts match the very vibrations of everything that you manifests in your life. So if you just simply "think" the crystals have the healing potential and keep your thoughts positive, the creativity and positivity of the stones will amplify those thoughts. If you have evil intent or bad vibes, it will amplify those.

Grounding stones are perfectly matched for empaths. Empaths have to go through so many emotional and mental ups and downs and need daily protection. They need that affirmation that they are worth more than taking care of everyone else's emotions and problems.

The clear quartz crystal has been on Earth since the beginning of time. Ancient civilizations have used crystals for many different reasons. They used them as jewelry, peace offerings and for protection. Quartz is a crystal that makes up 12% of the Earth's crust and is used very often in technology for things such as time keeping and information storage. Yes, Quartz is a kind of crystal and actually communicates through computers and this vibrational energy can be transformed through us as well. Yes we are also electrical beings. That energy and vibration we all feel when we walk across the carpet and then touch something like a door or a light switch is an electrical current actually flowing through us and then when we make contact with someone or something, it causes that small shock. We are all biological, spiritual, and electrical beings. The sun has a powerful electric energy that every creature, stone, crystal and plant needs in this world to survive and recharge. So yes energy is here is one of the key words when discussing crystals and the way that they connect with the earth and human beings.

The importance again when using a crystal whether you are an empath or someone interested in clearing out the negativity in your life, is your intention. Your thoughts. Keep in mind that your thoughts are what you end up manifesting into actions even if not directly. What we focus on and think about is everything. The crystals bounce of your thoughts, your overall energy. When you have a clear mind and purpose it provides insight into our dreams, aspirations, and values and that is what the crystals do for an empath.

The environment is especially important in order for crystals to form. The correct mixture of the elements is crucial as mentioned previously. The need of energy. The temperature, the light, water are all key factors in a crystalized formation. The color, size and shape are all a result of this process. Why is this important? Well like any other creature on earth, crystals are alive and full of earth's energy compatible with us as humans as we are also energy. Crystals work with the human energy field with the ability to diffuse, shift and or absorb energy. They vibrate on different levels as well.

Let us go into the different types of crystals that their are and how each one serves a purpose.

GROUNDING CRYSTALS & STONES:

Hematite Crystal -

A powerful stone that helps keep the body and spirit grounded. While all crystals have powerful and amazing grounding effects, the Hematite crystal stands out in its power to activate and clear the root chakra which is the energy center that anchors us to the earth and provides a feeling of balance and stability. It has the ability to absorb the toxic emotions that keep from enjoying life to the fullest and the negative emotions we absorb from others. Hematite is also excellent for healing the body because it cleanses the blood and supports circulation

Fluorite Crystal -

Fluorite jewelry is known to help neutralize and absorb any negative energy that may come into your energy field such as stress, anxiety, negativity, etc. It works as an energetic vacuum or tornado working to absorb and clean the energy of the body, spirit and mind. Fluorite crystals are said to magnify and amplify the power of any gemstone that touches it.

Amethyst Crystal -

- The Amethyst stone is a very powerful crystal. With it's abilities to not only heal and protect but be used as a spiritual energy source can really guide an empath. This crystal is one of the very few stones, with it's very unique and beautiful purple coloration, that is a form of quartz that contains iron and other minerals within it. It is a meditative and calming stone that promotes calm, peace, and balance. Since empaths have the unfortunate pleasure of taking on other people's thoughts, feelings and emotions, it only makes sense that they would get bogged down with depression, anxiety and stress. Stress come from anywhere and anyone. You need protection and guidance. The amethyst stone blocks mental stress and negative emotions.

- Has a beautiful violet color. It magnifies positive vibes all the while cleansing the body of negative energy when placed against the skin. It works as a natural stress reliever. It boosts the spirit and encourages spiritual growth by protecting the aura from damaging metaphysical debris and toxic emotions such as anger, anxiety, fear and more. The Amethyst Crystal is also an amazing tool for soothing the mind during meditation. When it comes to the psychic powers associated with the stone, it can vary per person and be vast.

The amethyst crystal, in many ancient cultures, was only accessed by the Kings, Priestesses, and Priest. It has been said by many that the stone can be used to awaken the third eye chakra and psychic abilities. That it has the mystery and key to enlightenment. It removes the baggage of the past and clears judgement therefore smoothing the path for your psychic abilities to work. You can't move forward or "see" forward if you are constantly looking back. It clears out regret in past lives and gives insight on the future.

- Greek mythology mentions the Amethyst stone in detail. There are different legends that are both moving and inspiring about this crystal. Greek mythology has a legend that the god Artemis turned a beautiful human woman named Amethystos into a clear white stone because she was begging for protection from the god of drunkenness and wine called Dionysus. He was chasing after with lust and desire that was overwhelming. When she became this stone now known as the Amethyst stone, Dionysus then poured wine over her giving honor to her. He was truly in love with her. This wine that poured over her now stone form, stained the clear white stone into the rich purple hue that the amethyst crystal has today.

Aquamarine Crystal -

Harnesses the power and energy of the ocean. This stone is an essential crystal in your healing collection because it helps reconnect us to the water and the earth. It was used long ago for good luck, protection, fearlessness and boldness. It has amazing soothing and calming effects and it said to be the symbol of eternal happiness and youth.

Aqua Aura Quartz Crystal -

Acts as physic bulletproof protection and or barrier. It gets rid of harmful energy trapped inside of you. This crystal can stimulate the throat chakra, therefore enhancing your communication skills. It helps provide inner truth about yourself that you may be searching for. With the nickname "Stone of the mind" it can increase your mental abilities. It can provide mental clarity and amplify your thinking. The Aqua crystal strengthens meditation which can enhance psychic abilities. It is used to empower and enhance clairaudience, telepathy, automatic writing, clairvoyance and physical healing.

Aventurine Crystal -

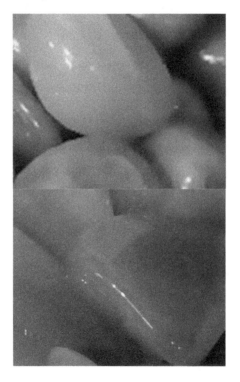

Is known as the "Stone of opportunity". It is said to be one of the most powerful gemstones for wealth, happiness, good luck and to manifest great prosperity.

It has been used to boost chances of luck in any situation. The color is green and many people use the color and or symbol for good luck. For example, while gambling or playing scratch cards. Saint Patricks day is centered around the color green as well and many believe that to be the day of good luck. Many times in history this color and symbolism has been used to create and boost situations for the better. It is the stone for optimism and helps you have confidence in new situations. Wearing one of these stones can help bring joy and zest in your everyday life. This gem is connected to the heart chakra and helps cleanse your emotions and heart chakra.

.

Azurite Crystal -

This crystal enhances intuition. It targets the inner vision and opens the mind and the third eye chakra. This stone expands the mind and opens you to limitless possibilities. While helping you realize your own potential it brings you closer to the universe and the divine. It clears away tension and confusion with ability to explore past or alternate lives and clear the throat chakra. It contains immense energy and amazing healing powers for disease and calms stress levels.

Black Tourmaline -

Do you see the shape and beauty of this crystal? It is so defined and formed perfectly. It has many qualities that would greatly benefit an empath. It is a rare and beautiful stone found only in Russia and was formed more than two billion years ago.

It contains *fullerenes* which are very powerful antioxidants that have amazing effects. Such as strong anti-inflammatory and antihistamine effects that in turn relieve body, muscle pain and improve the immune system. It is also a very helpful stress reliever. This crystal is connected to the root chakra. The root chakra is located at the base of the spine.

This stone has the ability to purify the mind of negative thoughts and feelings. Ancient magicians used the crystal to protect them from evil entities when casting their spells. Today it is known as the stone of protection and also has the ability to be used as a psychic shield, able to deflect negative forces, entities and emotions. It is also a powerful grounding stone, connecting you to the Earth. It has amazing effects on the hair and nails, soothes panic and anxiety attacks, and guards against radiation and electrical confusion within the body caused by radios, computers, cell phones, etc.

On a constant basis we are exposed to all sorts of radiation. Cell phones, offices, tanning beds, microwaves, laptops, tablets, earphones, etc. These gadgets release harmful radiation known as electromagnetic radiation. Prolonged exposure and or potent exposure to this can cause radiation poisoning and cancer. Among other things, symptoms may include diarrhea, headaches, nausea, dizziness, loss of appetite and rapid heartbeat. Being around huge amounts of technology, cars, and buildings can cause radiation, stress, and even anxiety. We use our phones everyday and most people keep them in their pockets which is very close to the body and making contact with the skin when we put it up to our ears.

The Shungite crystal can help guard against harmful radiation such as these and transforms the radiation into biocompatible energies. It almost acts as a filter. On an automatic fridge, for example, once you press the button the water will still go into a cup but there's a purifier catching the toxins first while the water is still heading into the cup. That is how the stone behaves when it catches radiation and turns it into positive elements more compatible with the human body.

The Bloodstone -

Is an intense healing stone used to cleanse and realign the lower chakras with the heart and is conducive to balancing the total body in order to overcome any distress or anxiety associated with re-alignment of these energies. It was once called the Sun Stone. Its energy carries the purity of blood and inherently speaks of birth, life, strength and vitality, passion and courage. It is a nurturing mother goddess stone and helps with mothering issues and helps in easing misunderstanding and difficulties in motherhood. The Bloodstone is a major boost to the immune system with the ability to ward off inflammation, cold, flu and infection. It stimulates dreaming and heightened intuition.

Citrine Stone -

Is the stone of light and happiness. It attracts wealth and abundance. It brings clarity of the mind and helps the thinking process. This crystal provides the ability to see what you want and desire and to manifest it. It activates the imagination and energizes the body.

Dumortierite Crystal -

Known as the stone of patience it has the ability to put out metaphorical fires in the heart before they can reach the mind. It helps to approach problems with a calm mind and head before getting too upset.

Blue Lace Agate -

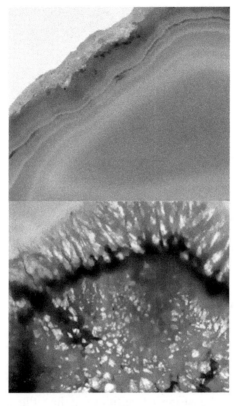

Is a stone of communication, calming, clarity and stress relief. It is connected to the throat and crown chakra helping to bring feelings of tranquility and alleviate anger and tension. It is the best crystal for stress relief and also has the ability to calm and soothe your pet.

Bronzite Stone -

This stone has the power to remove doubt and instill confidence. It strengthens your self confidence and self-esteem especially in times you may be feeling overwhelmed and or powerless. This crystal is a grounding and protective mineral that helps restore harmony in life. They inspire bravery and help you take responsibility for your actions.

Apophyllitie Crystal -

This stone creates a conscious connection between the physical and spiritual realms. It helps you recognize the truth in all situations. It is mentally and spiritually calming and can be used to open the third eye. This stone brings light and energy into the heart while releasing suppressed emotions. It allows for deep, relaxing and meditation.

Celestitie Stone -

This particular stone is found in geodes. A geode is a small cavity in rock that is lined with crystals or other mineral matter. They are hollow, almost circular rocks in which huge amounts of matter are secluded. The largest known geode in the world which also happens to be a Celestite geode, is located near a village in Ohio. South Bass Island, Lake Erie. Formed from warm solutions, they are found in rocks they often form in cavities such as sandstone or limestone. The term "Celestine" in French means "heavenly". Such a beautiful and rightfully given name.

It is known for positivity and has a gentle and calming energy surrounding it. They provide connection to the angelic realm and it promotes a pureness of the heart. It inspires deep relaxation and puts the mind at ease. It offers a healthy perspective on life allowing us to see our problems as guidelines instead of problems.

These are just some of the crystals among many that bring natural healing and happiness. That bring peace, confidence and greatly improve psychic abilities. Along with crystals and other oils and minerals of the earth, your environment is very important to your health and mental well being as well. One of the keys to protecting your emotions. Your home is supposed to be your place of solitude and peace. You want to make it as positive and loving as you can.

For those that have psychic abilities and a strong sense of intuition, I highly recommend this crystal. It enhances and boosts psychic capabilities. It connects to the crown, throat and third eye chakras making the messages you receive from the divine that much more clear. You gain access to a heightened sense of clarity and enlightenment so that you may tap into your powers clearly. Place the stone on your forehead or on top of your head, the crown chakra, and meditate with it. Let it connect to your mind and the spiritual realm. This will help you obtain clearer visions. It will also make your dreams more intense and vivid, giving you a way to remember them in great detail. Learn information in your dreams. Keep a small dream journal with you so you can write them down while they're still fresh.

One way to use this stone is by sitting with it in the palm of your hand and meditating with it. Let the vibrations and healing properties flow. Let your mind connect with its abilities so that it can enhance yours.

To keep out the negativity and calm your emotions, try a few of these things.

- *Meditation* - it helps calm the mind and helps develop the power of stillness. Practicing meditation is beneficial for so many reasons. It is used to train attention and awareness and achieve a mentally clear and emotionally calm state therefore helping you to develop calmer thinking and clearer actions.

- *Yoga* - is a practice that also involves a calmness and certain serenity that comes with it. It involves spiritual practices that connect the mind and body that bring you to a place of peace.

- *Writing* - writing can be so therapeutic. Taking the time to write down how you are feeling, your experiences, and emotions can be very helpful in cleansing the mind.

- *Sacred Space* - in your home, find a place or room that you can make your own "sacred space". A place where you can light candles, use sage, and meditate when you need to. Find a place where it is mostly quiet so you can think, study and learn your crystals, think, and breathe. I recommend everyone have a place of calmness and peace for themselves. The world can be a loud place and everyone needs somewhere to unwind.

- *Warm Baths/Water* - In the spiritual world, water is known for cleansing. The soul, the mind, and the body. Hot baths are very refreshing, energizing and helps purify the body as well as the soul. Sitting in water brings clarity to thoughts and cleanses your mind.

The earth provides so much for us to live at peace. Along with pets, such as cats or dogs, that bring comfort into our lives. Plants are another benefit to have in the home. They bring life and positivity to the atmosphere. They reduce carbon dioxide levels, reduce levels of certain pollutants, and keep air temperatures low. Plants are alive and people can feel that when they are in the home. They bring warmth and comfort to the earth. The sweet smell of a flower is beautiful and opens the senses. Pleasant smells lift the mood and morale.

Burning sage also has many benefits. It enhances intuition and is used as a protective barrier. It purifies and can be used to connect with the spirit realm. It also enhances alertness. Burning sage in the home can contribute to keeping away negative energies and evil intentions as well as toxic emotion and confusion.

Feel free to research and look up information on this topic and ways to relax the mind. Come up with your own approach to your new found abilities and incorporate them into your life. Include things that make you happy and things that clear your mind and help bring you peace.

HOW TO GUARD YOURSELF AGAINST ABSORBING OTHER PEOPLE'S ENERGY

It is all too easy for an empath to absorb someone's energy. They can simply walking past someone, touching them, and even talking to them. Being near them or in the same vicinity is also very possible. It has even been said that some have felt the energy of others miles away. Have you ever heard of someone saying they felt something major happening and perhaps saw a vision of it and then they turn on the news and that was indeed the event they saw or felt? Well energy and empath power can be that strong. You can begin to feel things from a far distance.

The crystals discussed earlier are extremely beneficial in this area. Having these crystals close to your body, close to the skin and in your home help shield you from ill intentions and negativity. They help protect you from the many energies people can unknowingly carry and pass on. That is the cycle of life. Energy is constantly circulated and recycled and if you want to guard against negative energy from others, these crystals and stones are highly suggested.

Avoiding places that you know make you uncomfortable is the best way to avoid overwhelming feelings of negative emotions. Prevention is the key to survival. An often spoken term but is seldom taken seriously. Instead of having to recuperate from an event, simply began to know yourself, your limits, boundaries, and places that you do not want to go because of how they make you feel. Others may not understand and may pressure you but do not let that stop you. Hold fast to your true self and though it may seem like you are being distant, you are just trying to keep a peaceful state of mind. Some people don't realize how unhappy they are because they have no boundaries. They allow whatever and whomever to come into their lives and their personal space. They go anywhere, even places that may make them feel a certain way, places that carry certain energies, and they are completely unaware of it.

You must know yourself and learn the things and places that may be too overwhelming for you. Another way to protect your mind and body against absorbing unwanted energies is to avoid engaging in toxic conversations and relationships. When you sense someone has a problem do not overly engage unless that person is actually asking for help or wanting to talk but take care not to become a target and or receptacle for negative energy as all energy needs an outlet. Stay clear of the area so it does not transfer and now you become the host of the negative and toxic energy.

It helps to keep in mind that you are not responsible for anyone's actions. You are not responsible for everyone's problems and you cannot save the world. There are many empaths that feel everyone's emotions and want to solve the world's problems and that can take a real toll on the person. You have to always fight the urge to help or save someone. You have the overwhelming need to metaphorically "stop and give money to every person holding a sign" but constantly tending to someone else and never to yourself can lead to depression and downfall later down the line. Focus on yourself and the things within you that you need to work on and try not to concentrate so much on the desires, fears, and problems of others. Being bold and taking a stand for your beliefs and your position on any situation offers a sense of honesty and cleansing. Getting out what you need to say with confidence helps release all the emotions you would have suppressed had you held your tongue and it clears the air of any confusion. It also lets the other person know that you are serious and holding your ground. That you will not receive the negative energy they are trying to transfer to you.

Finding ways to relax and calm your on energy along with avoiding others negative energy will put your life more at ease and you will find balance. Your peace of mind and mental stability are extremely important and mean your very survival as an empath. Find the things you like to do that teach you more about who you are and that teach you ways to find peace and calmness. Discover new ways you can protect yourself from toxic emotions and energies. Find the crystals and stones that best work for your soul and personality. Create your own reality and happiness within it and do not be afraid to set boundaries with anything that does not sit right with your spirit.

Section 3: Empaths & Employment

Keeping a job may sound easy enough and yes under certain circumstances for many, it is. But for those that have anxiety and for empaths it can be especially difficult. Everyday that you walk in to your place of employment, you are subject to feel what everyone around you is feeling. You also have the responsibility of the workload as well as the tasks of making sure you can keep up with the managers and bosses standards. That may sound like just an everyday occurrence for most. But for an empath, you are constantly burdened with others problems and emotions all the while taking care of their work duties.

You can feel the things your co-workers are feeling, possibly sense what they are thinking. All those thoughts and feelings bouncing around in your head along with your own for 8 to 10 hrs a day can be overwhelming.

There may be times when you are tasked with a group project that requires you to work closely with co-workers therefore providing more opportunities and closer proximity for you to absorb their energy be it positive or negative. Or perhaps your job may require mandatory overtime on top of an already stressful day. All those hours around people with problems of their own all inside them that they bring to work from home, from their friend's houses, they bring their relationship problems, all of it carried around with them and that energy is just waiting to be transferred.

Some people like to release their problems by talking and others just end venting and being mean to those around them as a way of release due to pent up anger. But that path normally solves nothing and yes we all need a way to release tension and stress but taking it out on someone else just isn't the answer. If you see someone come to work angry, chances are you should stay clear. If know them, sure you can try and help but if you are an empath I can guarantee that if you have to be around that person all day, you will absolutely end up absorbing all of that energy and then you will need a place to release it and the cycle continues. Break this cycle by forming the boundaries previously mentioned. Even if it gets to the point where you may realize that your place of employment is just too toxic and negative and you may have to find a new job if only for the sake of your mental health and overall happiness.

Sometimes a paycheck just isn't worth your soul. It isn't worth giving up true happiness and light in this world. Realistically, we all don't have the choice to pick and choose immediately what we want to do and what will make us happy when it comes to employment, so that may take planning. But there are some things you can do to help guard your emotions and protect your mind while you are at work.

- Carry grounding crystals

- Set Boundaries

- Focus on your work and less on those around you

- Practice meditation at home to better prepare you for the work week

- Find work that is more at ease with the abilities of an Empath such as:

Life Coach

Guidance Counselor

Massage Therapist

Writer

Nurse

Teacher

Social Worker

Nurse

Artists

Help other Empaths/Start support groups

- Find those who are positive at the workplace

- Stick to the work and avoid unnecessary dramas, toxic situations, and problems most people indulge in at the workplace.

- Remember that the power is always in your hands and if you do not like your current situation, then you have the power to change it. Never think you are not in control of what you want and deserve.

THE IMPORTANCE OF MORNINGS

The morning is the start of the day. The sun is peeking over the hills and you can start to hear everything outside come to life. Your mornings set the tone and pace for the rest of your day. Some people do care for breakfast that much but you should hydrate and snag something to eat because you want to have fuel for the day. If you wake up angry or tired and are also famished or malnourished and hungry, yor more prone to find negativity and be cranky then you are to have a good day. As empaths, knowing you have to go to work and be around a lot of unwanted energy can really dampen your mood so I would suggest this. As you are getting ready in the mornings, have some incense and or sage burning. Play relaxing music and or motivational tapes and videos. Set the tone and expectation of your day at its highest with positivity and motivation. Also get plenty of rest the night before so it does not interfere with your next day. Sleep can definitely affect emotions and mental state. Next, try sitting in your car on the way to work and try meditating and repeating positive affirmations. Command how you want the day to be and remember how real and important energy and manifestation is. If you say it and believe, then it will indeed be so.

Your co-workers may or may not know about empaths and energy. They may not understand the need to eat lunch alone because you can feel overcrowded by people but that is not for you to explain to anyone. You do not have to deal with anything that you do not want to. Set your boundaries, do not get lured and drawn in to day to day work drama, and maintain your peace of mind. I mention the practice of mediation and boundaries because there are many people who are empaths that have a hard to time keeping a job usually due to the overwhelming amount of emotions, energy and pressures that come with working in today's world. This is another case of needing to know who we are in order to know what we can and cannot handle. For an unaware empath, they be not understand why they are feeling all the emotions that they do and may not understand why they cannot handle certain environments. For aware and awakened empaths, they know what they can and cannot handle. Some simply just avoid the work scene altogether and become entrepreneurs. We are living in a new age where you are able to connect to social media and start your own business. There is always a different way and another opportunity, you just have to be awake and aware.

So on the subject of work and other public places, do not overexert or stress yourself for anyone's else's benefit. You are the one, at day's end, that has to carry all the emotions and feelings you come in contact with and as an empath you know the effects that can have on daily life. Pick your career as wisely as you would choose anything else for yourself and choose what works for you. What flows through you. We all have to start somewhere but to start somewhere implies that there is a finish so where do you want to end up? You don't have to still be or end in the same place you began. You just have to tap into your abilities and the universe. You just have to actually believe it.

What we do as a career or job field in life plays a huge part of our overall lives and future. We spend a great amount of energy and time at work, to make money and buy the things we need and want. The average amount of time per day at a job is usually 8 to 10 hours. After that, there is a few hours awake at home to do what we need to do and then we have to sleep of course, to function. Unless someone owns their own business or has extremely flexible hours, most of their time is spent at work and if you're going to be at work you might as well be doing something you love. Just because it's called work doesn't mean it has to feel like work. Empaths emotions are very fragile and open to others feeling and emotions. They mostly want to help and nurture people, animals, the earth and plantlife. Going into career fields like these will give you the chance to not only enhance and practice your abilities with energy and healing but will also allow you to live as an empath while doing what you love. Coming in contact with energy in ways you choose not those forced upon you in the everyday working system. Build and shape your own reality as you see fit customized to your abilities, your needs, and way of life. No matter what field you choose, remember to always guard your energy and never give more emotionally than you can afford to give.

Section 4: The Empath and the Narcissists

Relationships and love can be especially tricky for an empath. We want to be with someone but for us it is a tad difficult because we feel things on a more deeper and spiritual level. We see through lies even though we may tell our own. We hide our emotions while calling out other people to share theirs. We want everyone to tell us their problems while we bury our own.

An empath can perhaps come off as "too much" and "too caring" while at the same time needing space due to the amount of emotions and feelings they experience. This contrast can conflict and confuse the person that is in a relationship with an empath and can pose problems down the line if not addressed and discussed openly, honestly and without judgement on either side.

Being honest with your mate about the things you experience can prove beneficial for them and also for you as an empath. Knowing yourself again is very important. If you know yourself, you can then share with your mate who you are, what you experience and your deepest feelings. You will know your boundaries and what you will and will not be able to handle. Toxic relationships are one of the biggest causes of depression and broken hearts and to know which ones to avoid, you must know yourself.

There are two polar opposites that wind up together and rarely see the damages in that until it is too late. The empath and the narcissist. The definition of a narcissist is a person that is self absorbed. A person with an excessive interest and or admiration for themselves. Narcissists have a long termed pattern of self absorbed behavior, the need for constant admiration, and have an extreme lack of empathy for others while also thinking they know what is best for everyone. Now since empaths are natural healers and care so deeply for others it only makes sense that these two people are exact opposites. Narcissists care for themselves more than anything and the empaths feel and care about people more than themselves. So when this sort of couple comes together it can be the beginning of many problems. Narcissism also includes the ability to manipulate someone in order to get what you want as well as never taking responsibility for one's own actions. Narcissist tend to believe that they are "without sin" and that everything that happens is someone else's fault. It is very hard to be in a relationship with self absorbed, victim blaming individuals but it surely happens.

It is emotionally and psychologically dangerous for an empath to be involved in a serious relationship and or marriage with a narcissist. Because most empaths are so naive to their powers and do not yet fully understand what they are experiencing and are fully capable of, so they come off as someone who may be shy or extremely nice and you can tell them anything. They may be someone easily influenced and they sense and feel emotions and feelings toward everyone they meet, they wind up giving to much of that love, that benefit of the doubt, and healing to the wrong person. To a narcissist, they're direct opposite. Narcissists thrive on being doted on. They love attention and rarely care to give any back. They love and crave validation of almost any sort. They need to be the smartest in the room. They feel they need to be the most "different" person in the room so therefore they can stand out. Even if it's not with a lot of actions. All narcissists are not very talkative. Some aren't your typical "model" shallow type of narcissists. Some are just self indulgent, it's all about them and their feelings, and what they want. They are master manipulators.

So if a narcissist loves attention and being taken care of, and constant validation, what exactly does a empath do when in a relationship like this? They do exactly that. They give attention, provide constant reassurance and validation, and take care of the narcissists. See, people only do what you allow them, and empaths allow a great deal. We can carry a great deal of emotion for others. We easily place ourselves in their shoes and can relate to how we'd feel if someone did something nice for us so we overcompensate with that belief and we love hard. An empath is the perfect person for narcissist in theory because the empath never stops healing, never stops being who they are at heart therefore making it easier for the self- absorbed person to just sit back and let the empath keep stroking and building their ego in every way.

Emotional abuse can occur in any relationship but studies have proven that being in a relationship with a narcissist doubles those chances. Empaths and people all over the world are waking up and realizing their worth and you must do the same. Do not let you empathetic nature cloud your judgement and allow things you would not have normally tolerated. The best way to deal with a textbook narcissist is to not deal with one. There is no nice way to tell someone they are selfish. No matter how many words you use or ways you try and word it, if at the end of every day all they still care about is themselves, remove yourself from the situation.

Many assume that you have to be in a full blown physically abusive relationship to be unhappy and that is far from the truth. There is a such thing as mental torment. Mind games with very little action or effort to make the "nice words" a reality. That is all mentally and even physically exhausting and you have every right to move on to someone who does not have to play games with your mind and belittle you anytime you finally defend yourself and speak truth. It does not have to escalate to the point of physical abuse for you to be unhappy. You have every right to want the life you envisioned for yourself. You have a right to embrace the things you love uninterrupted by the negative words from a narcissists who only want you to stay around to take care of them. Not so they can love you. Not so they can take care of you.

Empaths are genuinely caring people and some people take that for granted. Narcissists especially. Please don't misunderstand, I am not saying that every person that has selfish and manipulative tendencies is a narcissist that is fully aware of what they are doing when they may hurt someone. That is not true. Some people just may need to see the light and the error of their ways. They may not even be aware that they are this type of person but make no mistake, though someone may be unaware of their toxic nature, it does not make it any less harder to cope with.

When in a relationship with a person who has the power of not only massive self confidence but the ability to manipulate and alter the mind, narcissists, it is imperative to know yourself and to set boundaries. If you are easily swayed into actions and easily influenced, then you can become a target for selfish, greedy, manipulating people. If you are someone not solidified in who you are, then you subject yourself to allowing the narcissists to tell who you are, what you're worth, and what you're capable of. Therefore creating a reliance on the narcissists for survival and validation. You never want to become reliant on anyone for that and especially a narcissists. They can make you believe you need them and only them to survive. That everyone around you will never add up to them and sadly they can make you believe that you yourself are nothing without them. That is when the isolating and estrangement of your family and friends finds its way into the situation and before you know it, the narcissists really is somehow all you have left.

Because you pushed them all away or they may have just distanced themselves because they see something that you do not see or have not yet wanted to admit.

In the spiritual world these sort of souls are called "energy vampires". Narcissists literally feed off the emotions and energies of others be it for the good or the bad. They survive by going victim to victim feeding off their very life force to go on. Now, remember for most textbook narcissists, it is about ego. It is about control. It is ultimately about them. So understand, that if that means putting you down, manipulating you, or belittling you and your every mistake so that they can build themselves up, they will certainly do that. They will do it to maintain their image, their ego and to fulfill that need to feed on someone else's pain, sadness, or misery. Again, an energy vampire. When a mentally abusive, rage fueled narcissists comes at you full force with their perfectly thought out words and harsh attempts to make you feel less about yourself, that is only to empower themselves. They are literally sucking your energy and using for themselves. You must never allow this. That is why the more you know about yourself and your powers as an empath, the better. That is why boundaries are extremely important. Everyone out there has a few selfish qualities or something about them that we all need to improve on but if you are with narcissists, you will absolutely have to have boundaries, there is no middle ground or debate on the topic. You have to be just as confident as them, just a brave, and just as willing to take what you want just as they are. Because that is what energy vampires do, they take and take and then blame you for having nothing left. So maintain who you are, do not give too much of yourself and your mind away to anyone, for time can never be replaced. State and maintain clear boundaries about what you will and won't tolerate and compromise on. Be just as firm in your actions as narcissist is always in theirs.

Rely on what you know about yourself whenever you feel self doubt creeping in. Rely on the use of the crystals that target the areas of the heart, strength, self-courage and confidence. Carry them with you, wear the powerful stone wristbands or rings for affirmation, and meditate and think about the life you have and the one you want.

Ask yourself these questions as well to further assess the position you are in your relationship:

Are you with someone that loves and understands the things that you experience as an empath?

Are you with someone that is selfish or someone that views your wants and desires just as important?

Is your life filled with happiness and upbuilding or is it full toxic energy, victim blaming, and emotional abuse?

Have you taken care of yourself as much as you have taken care of your mate?

Does the relationship feel completely one sided whether it revolves around one issue or all of them?

Can you embrace and develop your gifts as an empath with whom you are in a relationship with?

Can you be honest with your mate without fear of the argument being turned on you?

Do most of your discussions with your mate end with you at fault?

Are you somehow the only one always apologizing?

Are you the only one trying to carry the love and survival of the relationship?

Are you frequently belittled, put down, and told you are nothing without your mate?

That is a pattern with a narcissist that you have to begin to pay attention to. Pay attention to all the signs. Most of the red flags are right in our face and we put it to the side or create an excuse out of love. That does not do anyone any favors. After a while you begin to "wake up" and realize what has happened. You will realize just how different you really are due to the unhealthy relationship and its effects and you realize that it may not be best for your mental health and overall happiness to be with such a toxic person.

When picking who we want to spend time with or the rest of our lives with, we must choose with care. A narcissists may not truly see the harm in their actions and sometimes "love" can literally blind you from the obvious. As an empath, you feel emotion very deeply so you feel these emotions of loneliness and feeling different than everyone else, but you also love this person. You also feel sorry for this person. An empath sees the good in everyone even when others may think there is none. But you cannot continue to overlook harmful actions and words. Sometimes people think the words "sorry" can wipe things away and it just simply cannot. A narcissist has one hell of a way with words. That is primarily how they use their skill of manipulation. They can say words that cut extremely deep. Dealing with that kind of behavior can become what may seem normal but it truly is not, nor is it healthy and the moment it is normalized, is a big problem though it may seem like you have in under control.

Staying in a relationship like this can have unintended damaging long term effects especially for an empath who absorbs negative energy like a sponge. For empaths, it is not just "hurtful words". We feel the jagged edge of a knife that are indeed those words. Words are very powerful and while to some it was just a "bad conversation". For empaths it was an energetic and traumatizing shift to our psyche. We felt every emotion behind every harsh word. We can replay it like a movie and relive every energetic moment that happened. So we must take extra care with whom we let in our life, with whom we love and with whom we entrust our mind to.

Now obviously there are opposites that are together all around the world. There can be and are healthy relationships and friendships formed between an empath and a narcissists. Again sometimes your loving and selfless ways as an empath may show them the light and error of their ways and you two may grow as you get older but you must still know yourself truly. With people that are good at mind games, manipulation, and control like a narcissist, you have to have a strong mind and build that mental protection. You must know what you will and will not do and tolerate. You must stand strong in your truth and use the protective barriers such as grounding stones, crystals and sage to help with negativity and strong emotional shifts. Staying just as confident and grounded in your values as a narcissists will allow you to go toe to toe with them not be put beneath them. When you are an educated empath that knows about energy, are able to read people way beyond just the ability of recognizing "key facial expressions" and can control your environment and not let it allow it to control you, then yes the chances of having a healthy relationship with someone who is a narcissists or have narcissistic tendencies are that much more likely of surviving. Because let's face it, we can't always choose who our hearts will fall in love with but what we can do is make sure that we don't allow that emotion of love to bring us to ruin by simply allowing someone to do or say anything they want because we "love" them and are too forgiving as empaths.

Now, is the time you need to truly get to know yourself, get to learn about energy, different personality types and how all these things correlate. Your life will change for the better once *you* are the one that is in control of it. Not someone else. Some of us are so nice that setting boundaries or taking some time to ourselves to re-evaluate our own lives feels like we are being selfish but that is not at all the case and if you take a close look at a narcissists, they have zero problem telling a person when they are too close, telling someone when they need space, or when they just simply want to speak their mind and make something all about them. So do not think you are being mean when others are protecting their energy without worrying if they are offending you. You must do the same. As an empath I understand full well want to please everyone and fix all their problems, and wait on them hand and foot but as an empath I can also say, that road is a lonely one and not many people feel the same as I do. This is a rough world and I had to learn it the hard way. Not everyone is sweet. Not everyone will love you to the moon and back. Not everyone cares. So I took it upon myself to set limits and boundaries for my life, who I allowed into it, and so on.

It means your very mental survival to be extra careful in choosing your relationships. Choose someone that adds years onto your life not subtracts from them. Someone who brings joy and can assist in guiding you on your spiritual journey. Or at least traveling with you on that path. Take your time and do not rush situations and relationships. Let things flow and you will meet the people that are supposed to be in your life. You will have signs in your dreams. Coincidences no longer become such and fates intertwine. You will find who you need but first you must become what you need to be and achieve a higher version of yourself. You need to first love and respect yourself so that others are left no choice but to do the same.

Section 5: Your Health As An Empath

Having a clean and clear mind leads to a healthy body, or so it should be. It is not that simple, for anyone, but for empaths it is especially challenging. Our bodies react differently to trauma, stressful situations and negative events. An empath can literally become physically ill depending on the level of negative energy they were exposed to and or absorbed.

An empath must also take care with the foods and drinks that they consume. Some of the physical trials an empath has to cope with are digestive issues, stomach problems, migraines and muscle spasms. When overwhelmed with stressful emotions and situations, empaths may experience depression, panic attacks, chronic fatigue as well as possible drug and alcohol addiction. They may be more susceptible to sex and gambling addictions as well. Empaths experience a great deal of emotions, stress, and pain.

A person with an addictive personality has the chances of being an empath. Empaths need something to relieve the stress and emotional and physical burdens. They tend to attach to things that make them feel better and act out when under immense stress. Even things that may not be good for them. They are looking for something to numb the emotions. To numb the pain. But this can be a dangerous thing to do if you have no self control. If you have no boundaries.

Some empaths may be unaware of why they have certain reactions to particular foods or why they are more prone to addictions. You have to do your research and invest in yourself with knowledge. The more you know the better. The more you know what to avoid and what can help. Addiction, depression, anxiety and other illnesses and situations like this all have a source. There is a reason why someone may feel the need to self medicate on drugs, why someone may feel depressed. It may be guilt, loss of a loved on, regret, shame, it could be a numerous amount of things. For an empath, it could be these things listed and it can also be all the emotions and problems we run into and absorb from other people. That stress and burden of having others people's toxic issues into our lives and not taking care of ourselves can result in finding unhealthy ways to self medicate and cope with the overwhelming amount of energy and emotions. Since stress can be apart of an empaths daily life, picking up habits like smoking and drinking to calm the emotions and stress can be a very easy habit to adopt and twice as hard to break.

Activities like smoking are harmful to the body and mind. As you grow on your journey as an empath and become more aware of energy and emotions, you can begin to understand the need of boundaries, the need of peace and balance, the use of protection and grounding stones, etc. These things are there to help you live a more positive and balanced life therefore removing the need to self medicate or isolate yourself from others keeping you on a healthier track in life.

The food and drink is also important. There are just certain things an empath can't eat without getting an upset stomach. Avoid heavy meats and access sugar.

Sugar creates a lot movement and hyper behavior. It increases anxiety as well. So empaths must especially take care with the amount of sugar that eat or drink. Caffeine is in this category as well. Caffeine increases the heart rate and can cause anxiety spikes as well. As empaths, emotions are already firing on all cylinders and in all directions sometimes. We take in energy from many different places and walks of life and since all energy needs an outlet, that energy can come out in our home or on someone we love therefore disrupting our daily lives so the last thing we should do is amplify the anxiety and that confused energy with sugars, syrups and caffeine.

Enjoy life, of course but take care with the amount of meats, dairy and sugar that we ingest. The term "You are what you eat" is actually just that. You may not turn into a pig for eating bacon but you will have the possible lasting effects of whatever comes with eating pork. Your body is a result of what you put in it and the work you put into yourself, like exercise for example. Your mind is also a result of what you put into it so take care with thoughts that you have, the things you watch, do, read and say.

Your environment and surroundings be it people or places is also very crucial to your overall health. Being around a stressful situation and negative people can cause migraines. Toxic events can cause actual physical pain and illness. Avoid places that make uncomfortable and if you must go somewhere that you feel you may need a little more energy protection, wear your grounding stones and crystals. Repeat affirmations and manifest the reality of what you want to take place. Keep yourself and how you will feel at said event or place in mind as the key thing that matters. Not someone else's desires. If you are feeling as if you need to take a step outside, do that. Do not be forced to associate and mingle with people that you feel give you negative or bad vibes. Distance yourself as often as needed because your energy and health is just as important as anyone else's. Empaths often put others needs before their own and at some point it can affect your health and life. Be sure to put yourself first and if you cannot do that, at least make sure you are one of the people on your own list to take care of.

Drink plenty of water. The brain is made of 73% of water. Drinking it helps you focus, stay hydrated, stay alert and concentrate. Caffeine and energy drinks are known to give a quick energy boost but can cause a major crash just hours later therefore creating the need for another boost in energy. And that is how the cycle of being addicted or needing something starts. So avoid drinks like these and go for water as often as you can. Water increases your energy levels and helps you go throughout your day with much more energy and positivity. It supports optimal body functioning which assist you being able to complete more tasks throughout the day. The better you feel physically, the more you can get done. If you feel weighed down and tired from heavy foods and a lot of sugary drinks, you're less likely to get a lot done. Clear mind and body are one of the keys to a happy and productive life.

So what can you do with this information? Research recommended healthy foods and drinks for empaths and treat your body with absolute care. You are gifted vessel with rare abilities. You want to take care of yourself as best you can.

SECTION 6: THE ENERGY REALM

There are people in this world that think the earth was created by a big bang, others think it was created by a God. Many think it just developed and expanded over time and the list of theories can go on. One thing that is clear is that we are all energy. That everything is energy. We may not know the exact source from which we came but we are much more than just skin and bone. We are not just "human". Though that is the scientific and technical name for our species but we are all indeed much more.

We are advanced technological beings in biological form. We are energy and can harness it. Empaths are selected or gifted to be able to absorb and heal bad energy in this world. It is unpleasant at times, yes but someone has to do it. There has to be some sort of balance in this world. Everything has an opposite. Light, dark. Good, bad. Open, close. So with all the darkness and negativity that can fill this world, empaths bring the balance of gentleness, positivity, and love.

The energy realm that we are in is real. Believing in the unknown and the spiritual realm will help you truly understand what you experience. If you are a person who only believes in what you can see and explain then it will be a harder task to understand and develop your gifts. To truly understand the things you experience. You have to believe in the spiritual and energy realm. You have to believe in the unknown.

The energy we all possess can change and shift at any time. It can be based on feeling and emotion. Emotions too are energy. Energy is the food we eat, the things we drink, the places we go all have an energy inside them. The thoughts and feelings that people carry around with them is all energy. Empaths see emotions as energy. Can literally see it and feel it as if was in physical form. When we walk into a location, some empaths literally have the ability to pick up on past energy in that place. We have the ability to also see and feel energy as if you can reach out and touch it.

Many people aren't aware of the power of energy and words. Words are just as powerful as actions. We can feel the impact words have much more than the everyday person. For us everything involving emotion and energy is intensified. You can find ways to help cipher the good energy from the bad. You can create the reality you want around you by making sure your environment is cleaned of negativity and toxins. By making sure you have boundaries, firm boundaries about the things you do want and don't want out of life. By taking control of your journey and not letting others energy, desires and feelings become yours.

Having the belief in energy and the things we cannot "see" can expand our minds beyond the physical. It would assist in evolving our abilities by understanding more than just the basics we are taught about the world that we live. We are taught in school and in life that we are human beings, made of bone and blood that eventually die and return to dust. Those that believe in religion believe in angels and heaven. Meaning they believe that once you die, your soul lives on elsewhere. Most people don't read more into that but think about it, doesn't the implication of a heaven or a hell imply that there is just more than the physical realm? That there are more creations than just human beings and animals. Indeed, for those that are not religious, they may not believe in a particular religion but may still believe in the afterlife and the unknown.

Regardless of belief of where we all may go after death or wether we are alone in this world, one thing that we can all agree on is that we are more than just creatures that walk the earth for a time and then it just goes on and on. We are energetic beings all connected to one another. Everyone has a unique gift and purpose in this world. You have to find yours. We all have wave of frequency that we ride. Allow the energy you have within you and the energies you come in contact with to guide you on this energy wave. You will come in contact with energy completely contradictory to yours and those that better you. You will be presented with choices on how to handle the energy you will be surrounded with in your life and each event that we experience in this world is part of our story and journey.

A huge recommendation I have for an empath is to please listen and respect the energy you feel. That intuition and gut instinct we are gifted with. It will truly guide you. If you feel a situation is wrong or does not feel right, please listen and avoid either the area or the person you are may feel has a strong negative energy. We have to come to understand that we were given this gift and that you can actually use it to have a more guided and peaceful life. Having an extra "sense" and ability to foretell and or feel when a situation may go wrong is a bonus in an unforgiving and dangerous world. If you are not aware of your power, and go against the guidance of your gifts, you will always find yourself in situations you do not want to be. You will find yourself frustrated and confused by everything that you are feeling only due to not listening to your inner enlightened self. So again, do not take energy, emotions, vibes and intentions lightly. They are the very things that are "giveaways" or tell tell signs of how a situation or event is going to turn out.

Energy is a big part of an empaths life and embracing it, learning to decipher it, and protect yourself from the different kinds of energies will only serve to better your life and learning to develop your gifts.

SECTION 7: THE BENEFITS AND PROTECTION OF SAGE

To protect your home and your aura, burning sage is highly recommended and has been used for ages. Sage is a plant given to us from the earth. Used for many different reasons. Sage can be used for the following situations:

- Burning sage was once used by the Native American tribes for multiple purposes such as healing, clearing space, and for ceremony. As well as spiritual purification.

- Using sage on the body as well as in the home or office can be described as a deep metaphysical cleansing.

- The leaf is also used to make medicine, helps with digestive problems, bloating, gas, diarrhea, loss of appetite, memory loss, depression, and heartburn.

- Sage has been known to help relieve the symptoms of menopausal sweats and as well as hot flashes.

- Sage has anti-inflammatory effects.

- Sage can greatly improve your sleep. It contains magnesium which is a mineral linked to improving the quality and tranquility of sleep.

These are just some of the effects and benefits of using sage. This amazing plant contains small amounts of magnesium, zinc, vitamins and copper. It is a stable herb that belongs to the mint family. It is in the category of other herbs such as rosemary and basil. It is a natural cleaning agent. The earth provided so much when it provided us with sage and it definitely is fit for an empath. We suffer physical symptoms and exhaustion of emotions that absorb each day. Along with everything else that you may experience, depending on what type of empath you are, it can quite a lot.

We are in a world that comes with many temptations, trials, problems, events that can cause major change to our lives and without guidance and protection it can be difficult to survive in it.

Sage is one of the ways to keep yourself protected.

These are some of the looks of the plant. It comes in many different colors and shapes. There are also many different types of sage. Some are edible and have been used for chicken and soups and some sage is not. Others are meant for healing and inhalant more than a food item.

If you want to clear your energy field and the energies of others that you absorb burning sage is very beneficial. You can cleanse your home, your office, your car, anywhere you consider your personal space and place you have to be. Cleanse the air and the negativity that may be lingering. There is energy everywhere and sage can help cleanse it so that you can breathe easier and think clearer. It opens and purifies the mind and body.

The smoke from the dried sage can actually change the composition of the air and can have a direct effect on reducing stress levels. In order to cleanse your house for example, you want to make sure that the doors or windows are all open. Place the sage bundle in a ceramic dish of some kind and light one end of the sage and put out the flame. This will release the smoke. While walking around slowly, wave the smoke in all the corners and doorways. While the smoke is burning, keep reciting the incantation in your mind. When the area is clear, allow the sage bundle burn out on its own or you can do it yourself gently. You want to make sure that the doors or windows are all open.

This process will purify your home and or personal space and allow for positivity energy to flow within that area. The use of sage is for healing, and the smoke is used to bless, cleanse and heal the person or object needing cleansing. Everyone could use a refresh and restart. To feel clean and anew. Sage is like an energetic shower washing away toxins and negativity. For an empath, this is something that may be practiced frequently in order to keep a clear and peaceful mind. Keep your home and mind and the ones you love protected by any means. Find what works for you. Not everyone is into the use of sage but I do recommend it for its many wonderful healing and health benefits.

SECTION 8: DIFFERENT KINDS OF EMPaTHS

Empaths have a unique effect on the world. Along with the known ability to absorb energy and a strong sense of intuition, there are many different types of empaths that have different abilities that all bring something to the world.

If you are reading this, you have knowledge about the unknown and sufficient experience in things you can not explain. You have had several brushes with the spiritual world and may be conflicted inside about the things you feel. Now that you have come to understand that you are an empath, you must begin to understand that it goes much deeper than that. That there are great things about yourself yet to be discovered.

Looking up videos, books and information on this topic can be extremely beneficial. It can help answer questions about what you experience, the energy you are around, and will be able to tell you what type of empath that you are.

It is in every empaths nature to feel. For emotion to sometimes outweigh reason. Doesn't matter which kind of empath you are. We feel and absorb energy of all kinds. We have a heightened sense of communication and intuition. Let us look into the different kinds of unique and special people that are out there, all around us, providing healing and love to the earth. An empath can possess all of these abilities, just one, or a few. It all depends on the person.

The core focus regardless of an empaths abilities, is emotion and the energy surrounding it. Identifying intentions without the need of words is a skill among empaths. Energy is not just in words, it is in someone's entire aura and, their facial expressions, their hand gestures and things that go "unsaid". Energy is in the way we drive, we talk to each other, the way we work, eat, sleep. Everything. Emotion is energy in motion. It all ties in together and empaths are heavily affected by these said energies.

The sensitivity level can be off the charts with empaths and "star children". Star children are very angelic and sensitive. They have hearts of gold and special perceptive abilities. They are very sensitive to sound and tone of voice. They are more empathetic and aware and than most children. When they see someone hurting, they too feel that pain and emotion. They will have the overwhelming need to reach out and help the person even being so young. They too are heavily affected by emotions.

Empaths, healers and star children alike all have an attachment to energy, nature and emotion. They are very attentive when it comes to other people's feelings and they can sense energy as clear as you can see the sky. As sure as you can breathe in the air. That energy tells the empath everything that they need to know. Energy, among many things, is information and or it carries information. For example, if you are feeling upset, that is an emotion, an event of emotional information or energy being expressed in the form of anger. Even without words, empaths can pick up on this energy the same as they can with positive energy.

Determining which "type' of empath you are, I feel, heavily depends on the things that you are drawn to. The situations you constantly find yourself in and the people you somehow find yourself around even if they aren't the people you wouldn't have ever chosen personally for yourself to call friends or family. I feel it is in your day to day life, actions, and overall purpose on earth. You can even find the answer in what your true calling or career path in life may be. Are you drawn to animals? Are you drawn to nature? Other people and their problems? Do you feel the need and desire to heal?

Well, let us talk more about that. These questions are posed for the purpose of finding your true passion in life and what type of empath you are. We will go into all kinds and details about them. Such animal empaths, intuitive empaths, earth empaths and so on.

If you are someone who is naturally attracted and drawn to nature and plants, you may be what is called a "plant empath". They are able to communicate with nature and plant life on a level unlike many others and the list goes on for the others as well discuss thoroughly in this book.

When you find yourself in situations that are toxic and negative, perhaps your healing abilities and empathetic approach and perspective can change that negative environment. Maybe there is a reason you were put in *that* family or *that* relationship where it seems like only sadness and negativity dwells. Your light may be exactly what is needed in places of darkness. Again, trials and situations like these are moments where it is a good time to consider if you have more to offer. If this is your purpose. Empaths often attract wounded people and narcissists. People who need someone to either listen and "heal" their problems and others that just want to take out all their problems on them because they are kind, soft hearted, and narcissists may believe they are easy to manipulate usually because empaths tend to want to save to the world and people please. Even to a dangerous fault. With being an empath comes the need for boundaries. You have a very big heart and not everyone will treat it with respect or treat you in the same manner. You have to learn to protect yourself, your energy and your heart. For empaths, the heart chakra stands out the most and must be protected because we feel so very deeply.

An empaths energy is always at risk, if you are either inexperienced or do not have energy protection, such as crystals and mental clarity, sense of self, and knowledge of self. SInce being an empath also includes absorbing others energy, not just people, this could be animals, plants, solar, you are at risk for not only absorbing negative energy but also taking it on. Living with it and it can affect your daily life. And I mean actually absorbing someone else's feelings. Have you ever been around someone or walk into a certain room and all of a sudden feel angry? When nothing is wrong? Yes, that person or that area may have negative energy and you, the empath, have now absorbed it. That is not your feelings, that is someone or something else.

Trips to the grocery store can be so overwhelming because of the amount of people you are coming in contact with. All those lives, stories, and emotions can be a lot to handle. With all the constant transfer of energy when you touch an item on the shelf someone else has touched. You can pick up on the energy of the person when you touch the item after them, therefore possibly transferring that energy into you upon contact. When you are exchanging money with the cashier, you are now taking in his or her energy. In truth, every human and living creature that makes contact transfers energy like this everyday. But for empaths, it is on a much more heightened and aware scale. That is why it is important to have those things that can help protect you from negative energy and unwanted feelings that may belong to someone else.

Yes, some of this may sound far fetched to many but to others they will know exactly what I am talking about. This is not far fetched, in fact, the more a person thinks simple and or small minded, only believing in what he can physically see, will always remain simple and or small. In order to determine your path in life or truly believe in anything you have to first drop all guards and open up the doors of possibility.

If you are unsure about where you may fall when it pertains to what kind of empath you are, do not be discouraged. This is not written law and there is not a certain category that anyone falls in but there are different and unique abilities per each type of empath, that they can possess and it helps to really invest in your interest and the things that you feel. At any rate, you are still an empath and the core common things all empaths have in spades regardless of what kind they are emotion and energy. We all flow with those laws. We respect them and how they work and we are connected to everything through energy. We do not need words to define a situation, rather we rely and listen to energy and intuition. We are all natural healers that have extremely empathetic hearts. With that being said, hopefully with this new information, you can discover what type of empath you are and expand upon it. Develop it and become the greatest version of what and who you want to be.

Section 9: Earth Empaths

Earth empaths are keenly aware and in tune with planet earth. They are in touch with the weather and can feel when changes are coming. The tides of the ocean and the lunar effects of the moon take an especially unique effect on an earth empath. You can feel the power of a thunderstorm or may even sense it days before it approaches. You may smell the change and moisture in the air, the difference in the animals, and so on. Earth empaths also feel and respect the intense power of the sun.

Most empaths can feel the energy of people where as an earth empath feels the energy of the earth and everything it has to offer. The waterfalls, pools, and baths have an energetic, cleansing, and powerful effect on them. They absolutely love nature and everything about it. They prefer to be outdoors more than inside.

Stargazing can be healing especially for an empath. Being in the sun and communing with nature can be restorative. When something happens to the earth you can feel it in your bones and when you are around a dirty place maybe a place that trash on the ground everywhere or pollution, can make you physically sick. That is not the case for every person, there are actually people who live in these kinds of conditions but for an earth empath, it can be truly difficult to see the earth harmed and polluted. You may get the overwhelming feeling to save the earth and want everyone to clean and respect it the same way you do. Sadly, the world isn't always kind to the earth and that can be emotional for earth empath. Wildfires, Forest Fires, and other horrific events can be very troubling for this empath due to their deep attachment with the earth, feeling her pain if you will.

Earth empaths have strong emotions and dreams about natural disasters and floods and may feel them even as they are taking place. If you have experience this feeling and have been wondering why you are always thinking about terrible events, tornadoes and destruction, this may be why. You are feeling the earths pain as well as what others may be experiencing in that location.

A few suggestions for earth empaths to find peace and balance in this world is to begin with trying to connect with the earth. You have this ability for a reason. You are here to communicate with and protect the earth. Of course no one person or human being can save everyone, stop natural disasters, or actually protect the entire earth but what you can do is help care for her. Treat the earth as best we can. To love and use what it has given us to survive but not abusing it. Keep it clean and try and keep our energy clean as well.

Yes, the earth can feel and cleanse away negative and toxic energy. The ocean is therapeutic as well as spending time in the forest, on the beach and any time that you can be in nature can empower your gift as an earth empath. The more time you spend connecting to the earth, the more you will understand about yourself.

The solar flares and the things that take place in the cosmos up above, or in space, can affect an earth empath as well. A solar flare is a sudden flash of increased brightness on the sun. Understand that the sun sustains and affects all life on earth so any changes that occur with the sun will surely affect all humans but especially in earth empaths. The sun affects the weather, our human bodies and minds, the seas and oceans, and affects our atmosphere. There are studies that have shown the direct link between solar and lunar events and the timing with humans and depression, suicides, episodes of bipolar disorder and more. Though it may seem like the planets, stars and moon are all very far away but we are all each connected to them.

The moon can also affect our moods and our thinking. Studies have also shown the effect that a lunar eclipse has. They take place rarely throughout time. The lunar eclipse can lead to some psychological episodes, depression, manic episodes and can change your thought pattern and actions during, right before and right after an eclipse. For an empath, an eclipse can cause some strange sensations and bring about intense emotions. They can feel the intense shift of energy in the air. They feel the tides in the ocean swaying this way and that. They feel the subtle change in the wind and with the animals. For many an eclipse is just this rare event where the sun is blocked for awhile by the moon and it only happens here and there throughout time. But there is much more happening during an eclipse. This is where understanding that you are more than just human and where you understand that you are connected to the earth, moon, planets, and stars more than you may know.

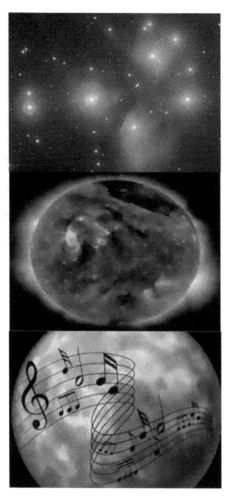

The earth has an energy field surrounding it at all times and it assist us in handling emotions, logic, and decision making. This field of energy helps humans and animals regulate our existence. There is a constant flow of energy within this field and when that energy is interrupted or altered in anyway, say for instance, an eclipse, when the sun is blocked, the moon and planets are moving and the flow of the cosmos is changing, that flow of energy can shift. Causing the mood swings, headaches, unexplained bouts of depression and suicides. Many empaths have come to understand that the energy shift that occurs during an eclipse is to bring things to the light. To put a stop to old habits and give birth to new actions, better decisions and a clearer path ahead.

An eclipse can be life changing if you allow it to be. They have the power to completely shift the energy on earth and brings things to the surface that has been suppressed and needs to be revealed and healed. For an empath, an eclipse can be exhausting and taxing on the body due to the amount of intense emotions that you feel from you as well as all those around you. The entire earth is going through a major energetic pull during an eclipse and you can feel all those things as well as the energy shift within the earth itself. Remember as an earth empath, your biggest connection is with the earth and nature.

Allow yourself time to heal after such climatic events, humble yourself to the power of the universe at this moment and listen to the energy you feel after an eclipse intently. Do not continue down old roads and bad habits. An eclipse is meant to shake things up and based on research and self experience, it most certainly does. But it is all for the best.

The earth and universe know exactly what they are doing and we are all connected to them. But in order to know these things, you must first learn them. You must dive into the things you feel and see. Learn as much as you can about the earth and yourself. For an earth empath it is best not to harden yourself against the things you feel on earth. Open yourself up completely. Open your chakras and allow yourself to feel and sense everything. From the animals to the energy in the air.

A career, hobby, or profession that an earth empath may love is practicing earth medicine, and or a botanist. A traveler or an explorer. These can bring happiness into your life while you get to connect to the earth and help keep her safe and cared for. The earth is your source. Learn everything you can about her and connect with the earth on a deeper level.

When it comes to practicing and developing your abilities, you want to first begin with connecting to the very source of your "power" which in this case is the earth. Again, going into a field or profession that involves the things you love and are connected with is a smart and positive way to practice and use your gifts with nature. If it is to tend and nurture animals, then develop hobbies that involve time with animals.

If you enjoy hiking and exploring the earth, do this as often as you can. Experiment and practice your gifts in the elements of nature. For example, try being outside and sensing a storm before it approaches. Really look at the clouds and notice the change in size, color and smell in the air. Notice the animals take shelter before it arrives. Really become involved in each and everything you feel when in nature and in the sky.

Meditation while in the wild or in nature is very beneficial and calming for the mind as well. You close your eyes and you hear no cars, horns, or sirens. You only hear and feel nature. When in nature, you learn to respect it and all within it. During meditation, listen to the sounds, the birds, the creatures that you hear. Awaken and develop your senses by listening to each sound and taking in each smell. Listen for running water nearby, that may be a stream. Listen for rustling in the trees or bushes, it may be something nearby. Connect to any water such as lakes, rivers, and oceans. Water is one of the greatest elements on earth. Water is also very soothing and calming for the nerves so swimming, sitting by water, fishing, boat riding, and meditating near water are very beneficial activities for empaths.

SECTION 10: TELEPATHIC

EMPATHS

A telepath is someone with the paranormal ability to read others' thoughts. Empathy is often paired with the ability to pick up on information and energy through taste, touch and smell. A telepath and the abilities of an empath are almost hand in hand. An empath can "feel" and have intuition about a person or a situation and an emotional transference of energy whereas a telepathic empath can have the ability of *thought transference* and are capable of reading thoughts, not just feeling the energy.

This may sound like it is impossible and if you believe that then it will be just as hard to learn yourself and your capabilities and just as hard to become all that you are able to be. Telepathy can be considered another level of empathy or a gift within a gift. Telepathy is not only mind to mind communication but can also be in dreams, images, and pictures. With the gift of telepathy you are given access to knowledge that is not physically and directly offered in this reality. These events can be from past, present, and or future.

Telepathy also known as (ESP) extrasensory perception, is the direct communication of two beings that is void of written and or verbal communication. It is the ability to transmit words, images and emotions to someone else's mind.

Now this may sound like something from X-men or some other superhero movies and there isn't much "physical" proof that telepathy exists but every idea and or movie comes from somewhere. Dating back to the late 70's, when the first Star Wars movie premiere hit the hollywood scene, we've been introduced to other foreign like creatures and inhuman powers. Such as "the force" which is actually "telekinesis". An ability to move an object without coming into physical contact with it. There have also been tales from tribes about humans with special powers among us. This topic goes back to understanding and believing in what many would call "impossible". The things an empath can experience are rarely in physical form.

If you are a telepathic empath and would like to develop your gift, take a look at some of the tips and images below.

1) *Concentrate* and *Focus* your thoughts. Covering your eyes (glasses,goggles) and or closing your eyes helps tune out the physical world and assists you in tuning in to the spiritual world so you can concentrate on the telepathic message you are practicing.

2) *Stretch* the muscles. You will need a lot of mental focus so having a relaxed and calm mind and body will clear your path as you try and tap into the unknown. Stretching increases blood flow in your muscles and is amazing for stress relief. If your stress level is up and your muscles are tense, it will be more difficult to concentrate and have peace of mind during meditation. Practice stretches and light exercises such as these before meditating so that you can balance your energy, stretch your muscles, and bring your mind to a calming state.

3) *Meditate.* Practice focusing on a single thought. Meditation helps clear the mind and heart chakras giving you a smooth and uncluttered path to the spiritual realm. Mediation helps control anxiety while bringing mental clarity and balance. Since telepathy is a mental power, again telepathy is the ability to communicate with people and animals without using words but by means of mental energy and intent transferred from one subject to another, the mind must be at peace and cleared. Meditation opens the chakras giving you the ability to receive information from the universe more fluently and gives you the power to really focus on your ability.

4) *Visualize* the person you are attempting to communicate with.

You need to picture the person in your mind as clearly as possible. Picture them receiving this message. Picture exactly what you want to say. Remember the feelings you have when you are with that person and imagine them right in front of you. Picture the connection you have with them.

5) ***Keep it simple.*** Start off easy. Don't try sending anything long or too difficult. Try imagining a simple word or phrase. Think of something that you want to tell the person you are trying to connect with telepathically. Think of a simple object or image very clearly in your mind. It helps to be extremely relaxed and in the environment to practice this.

6) *Transfer the Image* **or message to the receiver.**
Imagine the message actually leaving your mind and
entering the mind of the receiver. Try not to dwell on
it over strain yourself trying to concentrate. Relax,
think of the image or message and release it to the
receiver. Imagine the feelings of the person you are
communicating with. Imagine them actually receiving
the message. It must be real to you.

It helps if you, have someone to practice this with and not just picture a random person and sending them a thought. Practice meditation and calming the mind. Practice focusing on objects. Focus on your concentration and your breathing. For empaths, this can be particularly tough because we feel everything and depending on the type of empath you are, it may always be loud at times. You can hear thoughts, you can hear desires and literally see energy. But find a quiet and trusted environment where the energy is clear and you can practice meditation, yoga and clear thinking.

You can bring your gifts into the real world and develop them. You have unknown and untapped capabilities, you just have to believe and search for them. Research and consider all possibilities before you settle on a belief. Do not blindly follow and do not shun the gifts you were given. Telepathic empaths have the ability to read and hear the thoughts and mental faculties of others. To feel their pain and feelings. The ability to understand someone in a way that they may not understand themselves.

Empower yourself by learning all you can and using the gifts you were given to add happiness and help others in this world.

ANIMAL EMPATHS

An animal empath is someone that is able to keenly and internally understand and recognize the emotions, feelings, and mental state of an animal. This is actually more common than we may realize. Have you ever had a pet that you considered to be much more than just the house animal that you take care of? That may sound bad but some people may have pets but they just feed them, play with them but that's as far as it may go.

For others there is a true connection between their spirit and the animal world. They feel the pain of creatures that are hurt. They are utterly repulsed by animal abuse of any kind and they feel for them on a very emotional level. They want to save every animal and thinks even the "scariest" ones to them are gentle creatures viewed just like the others.

Some empaths prefer the company of animals to the company of human beings. They appreciate and respect the gentleness and natural instinct of nature that animals have. They respect the laws of boundaries and nature that animals heed to. Animals are very much in tune with the earth and nature. With the stars and the weather. Have you noticed when a storm is coming or when something bad is about to happen, the animals react to it? They may howl, bark, the birds began flocking to safety squawking their warnings to one another. This is because they are aware and intune with the cosmos and aren't polluted with constant distractions that humans have preventing them from achieving this level of awareness.

Another distinct difference between man and animal is that the animal hunts when it needs to and yes many species prepare for the winter and may store food for their young but it does not go beyond that. They do not crave to the point of excess. We as humans tend to need way more than we need for the basic comforts in life. We can be more concerned with material happiness than mental happiness and enlightenment.

For an animal empath, they naturally have this love and connection to nature and animals. They are able to sense the thoughts of an animal in ways others are not able to.

Animals heightened sense of awareness makes them extremely cautious when it comes to whom to trust. They do not trust all humans. An animal empath has been said to be able to use telepathy to communicate with animals and assure them that they mean no harm. Animal empaths have been found all throughout history in different cases and the view of this ability has been changed over time. They were not always viewed positively and were not always viewed negatively.

Many ancient priests believed that this ability was the work of the Devil and the occult. Others believed it was a gift and used for the good. For the protection of villages and the ability to help bring healing and peace between man and animal.

This skill is demonstrated by many in the world that have found a way to use their gift. There are several *careers* and *hobbies* you can take up in this area to help develop and expand your gift. Take a look below.

Career & Hobby Suggestions for Animal Empaths:

- Zoologist

- Veterinarian

- Nurse

- Animal Trainer

- Veterinary Assistant

- Animal Nutritionist

- Pet Sitter

- Animal Shelter

- Marine Biologist

- Going on safari tours

- Taking walks in nature

- Open an animal shelter or volunteer program of your own.

HOW TO DEVELOP YOUR GIFT

In order to develop your abilities you want to be sure that you are in connection with your chakras. You want to make sure that your crown chakra is open. There are crystals and stones such as the agate and amethyst crystals that can aid you in this. Make sure the mind is clear and you are at a state of peace. Practice this daily. Meditation and seclusion. Finding an area that you can focus and train your mind.

Once your mind is open and chakras are clear, make sure you are also taking in nature. Be around animals and your pets as much as possible. Do not force this however. Remember that animals do not trust everyone. If you have that natural gift and calling to them then yes please answer it. But do not put yourself in danger trying to prove anything or assure yourself of something. If you truly have this gift, allow yourself to be around the creatures and animals that bring comfort to your spirit.

Taking walks in nature, trips to the zoo and museums, spending a great deal of time with your pets will help develop your bonds. Try and understand your pet's emotions and feelings. Go past the routine of feeding and bathing them and try and actually hear their thoughts. Try to put yourself in their shoes. Develop the line of communication with animals by trusting both your instincts and theirs. If you are out in nature and it is not your pet, but a wild animal, take your time and do not rush or pressure the animal.

I get a lot of random animals that are normally "unfriendly" to others that just want to be next to me. I've had animals come up and trust me without having ever been around me. I don't overly talk when approached by a random dog or deer. I just stand there, and do not make direct eye contact. I open myself up to the animal and try to understand everything they have been through. The world isn't that kind to the animal race. I feed them and love them. I respect their laws of nature. In many groups, be it monkeys, bears, or wolves, the law is to never look them in the eye and never try to establish your own dominance, especially if surrounded. That isn't the time. When developing the gift of an animal empath you must leave ego at the door.

Yes you need self-confidence because you will need it, the wild and nature can smell fear, but you do not want to take it past the point of confidence. You must respect the animal and their space.

Now when confronted by an animal out in nature, this is where having your crown and heart chakras open is very necessary and beneficial. If you are open and enlightened the animal will sense that energy. Animals as we discussed have a very heightened sense of awareness and can sense bad weather and evil energy a mile away. They will not even approach you if something feels off or if you have a bad intention. They may not notice it at first and that is how many have fallen into traps but for the most part, animals are extremely aware of their surroundings especially if a human is around.

You want to make sure you have a positive and vibrant energy. It will radiate around you giving off approachable and gentle vibes. If you have a career that provides a way for you to be around animals, you should take full advantage of that. Practice your communication and healing.

Animal empaths are here to help protect, communicate with, and nurture the animal species in a cruel world that uses them for everything from food to the coats that people wear. Fulfill your mission by keeping them safe, healing them and dig deep to understand their emotions.

SECTION 11: MEDIUMSHIP

EMPATHS

Mediums and psychics are known for the ability to communicate with the other side. They have the ability to connect to the unknown world and receive answers from those that have passed on and those that exist in other realms. Not all empaths are mediums and not all mediums and psychics are empaths. The gift varies. There are empaths with this ability to connect with beings on the other side as well as feel the emotions that the person felt.

A medium empath uses their psychic or intuitive abilities to see the present, past, and future by tuning into the energy surrounding that person. That energy will tell them what they need to know. The energy, to a psychic empath, can be picked up as images and scenes from a movie. A psychic empath can walk into a location and pick up on the emotions and feelings, even images, of the past and sometimes they have visions of the future as well without having to be in the location of where the vision takes place.

Now this power may sound far fetched and hard to believe but it is very possible. This ability falls under the category of *Clairvoyance* and *Clairsentience*. Clairvoyance is the skill to perceive things or events in the future beyond normal or ordinary means. Clairsentience is the ability to just "know" something without being told. It can be described as a strong sense of intuition. This ability has actually been used to find missing people and lost objects. It comes with the power of being able to *divine* where someone or something is without any logical or physical explanation.

A psychic or medium empath can both sense and feel the situations and events of the past and present and most cases the future. This ability can be developed, it can be nurtured and it can be used for good. For this ability, it helps to research as much as you can. Find crystals that coincide with this unique gift, and find ways to practice it.

Began to keep a journal of the visions you have and write them down. I know for a fact that this ability can be difficult because for an empath it is hard to differentiate our own feelings and images from someone else's that we absorbed but taking the time to write down the things that you see in your mind will help you have a written reference to go back to and compare with the events that actually end up happening.

There are times I wished I'd done this but I couldn't tell that I'd had a vision until it was too late and what I saw was actually happening in real time, but how was I supposed to tell someone that or even try to describe it? Kind of hard to do unless you know someone that experiences the same things that you do. Or if you have a journal. If I had it written down and dated when I saw it, I could have something concrete to go on.

So that is what I started to do and I highly recommend it.

Something else that helps tremendously in this area is meditation. Calm your mind and try and listen and feel everything around you. Once you develop a state of stillness, you can begin to fill the vibrations of the energies and of the earth. Literally feel the crown chakra open up and achieve a heightened state of enlightenment. Being open removes the mental negative blocks that would prevent you from feeling all the emotions and performing the skills you are capable of.

A psychic empath has extrasensory perception. An extra sense if you will. An added ability outside of the uses of the five senses. We are taught that we all have five senses which are taste, smell, touch, hearing, and sight. A gifted person has more. The ability to "know", feel, and communicate beyond the ordinary sensory perception and means of communication.

In addition to meditation, crystals, and along with keeping a journal it is imperative that you keep your feelings and emotions separate from others. You want to keep your channel clear of any interference.

There are *Clair- (clear) cognizant Empaths* as well. This too falls under the category of a psychic empath. Claircognizant means a person with an ability to simply know things about the future and a person. They have the ability to pick up on deception and lying instantly. They immediately know when false information is being presented. They have the ability to solve problems and assist people with clear ways and understanding of how to solve their problems.

When an empath touches an object, he or she may begin to receive information based on the energy from the object. They may begin to see images of who owned it, touched it, the things and places that this object has seen.

Bring your awareness to a higher level and challenge yourself mentally. Push yourself and your limits spiritually and began to believe in more than what you can see. Taking walks and embracing nature helps get more in touch with the cosmos. The stars and moon are great sources of information and are held in very high regard. Look to them for energy and answers. Look to the books and resources that are available all around if you search for it. Those that seek and find.

This is a unique skill that takes much practice but if you are truly gifted, and you already experience these things, such as strong and intense gut feelings, the ability to just "know" information about a place or person, you may hear voices in your head and or see strong images in almost video like form that actually take place in real life, then you already know the power it has and you know you have the capability to use it. Please do not misunderstand, I do not mean actually hearing voices but more like a deep inner guiding voice that tells you the things you need to know. Listen to that guide, trust it. It's almost as if it's a very strong energy that you can see and hear that is given those who have opened their minds to their gifts and capabilities.

Mediums use cards, guided by the spirits to help them come to certain conclusions and helps them "find the light" when others need help in times of darkness. They use them to communicate with the other side and determine things that have happened and events that will happen. Others may rely on their sense of intuition and their heightened sense of awareness of people and their energy to tell someone something about themselves and the future they may see for them.

The knowledge and awareness of body language and a person's energy tells a lot about them. A medium is able to receive information from a source "unknown" to the physical world. They practice spirituality and come to a realization that they are more than "human" and use meditation. They're gift of intuition becomes heightened and they are able to use that to their benefit.

Discover what makes you comfortable and what tools you are comfortable using in order to progress and develop your skills. You will find that you are capable of more than you think, even in this "physical" existence. You must think outside of that box and see that the universe is much more.

DREAM EMPATHS

Dream empaths actually exists and go by different names. A dream empath is a person that has intense and lucid dreams that often have messages attached to them intended for the physical realm in which we all dwell. Let's talk a bit about dreams. Most people wake up and do not recall their dreams. They often have difficulty trying to recall a certain dream.

Have you ever noticed this problem? Maybe you remember some of your dreams and that is based on how they made you feel but have you ever wondered why it is that we cannot remember a dream we perhaps just woke up from? That is a mystery to many. The way it is just wiped from our minds we when awake it is almost as if we are not meant to remember our dreams, from beginning to end, down to great detail. Not unless you are a dream empath with a deep connection to unknown dream realm. Dreams are also not a continuous "day and night" scenario like it is in the physical world. The dream state is very creative and defies all laws of gravity and physical existence.

Dreams are a series of images, ideas, emotions, sensations, fears, and desires that occur in the mind simultaneously and involuntarily during the stages of sleep.

Sigmund Freud was one of the first psychologists to really study dreams. He believed that a person's dreams represent wishes that the dreamer subconsciously wants to come true. He also believed that thoughts, feelings, and memories are represented by concrete objects and symbols in a person's dreams. There is a strong connection between this world and the dream world. That is why we see familiar faces all the time or go to places that we've been before in this world in our dreams. But the true meaning and definition of dreams are unknown. What is known is the power of a dream. The feelings and emotions when you are asleep are just as real as if you were awake.

When you have a nightmare, you remember exactly how that made you feel, it perhaps shocked you and woke up you swiftly. Over time, humans have simplified what sleep and dreams are but we tend to underestimate what happens to us when we are asleep. How real pain or sadness feels when you are dreaming. Have you ever woken up crying, scared, or in a panic? Even said the words "that felt so real'. That is because in "another world" it was indeed real. We may not have a scientific explanation for dreams but we cannot deny what we feel and the creative and spectacular things you can only do in the dream world.

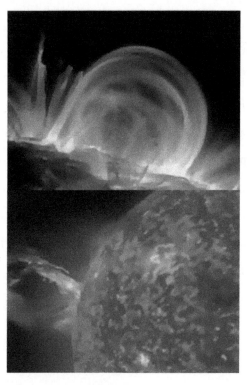

Now that we have briefly discussed dreams, let's tie it into the topic of an empath. Dream empaths have the ability to recall with great detail their dreams and are provided guidance on how to interpret them. They are also able to live their life more through their dreams. Though everyone has nightmares and may recall a dream, an empath will tie that dream to an actual life experience be it past, present or future. They are more connected and in tune with the conversations and images they receive in the dream world. They may notice more than the average person when it pertains to dreams and everyday life.

Empaths may live the dream more vividly than others. They may recognize more familiarity between the dream world and the physical one. With this ability, a dream empath may be able to help improve their current physical life with the messages and events that take place in their dreams.

They may receive warnings perhaps strong feelings of future events and signs about those around them or someone they are going to meet in the future. Yes, it is possible to actually see someone first in a dream and then meet them. With the ability to have vivid and divine dreams and actually remember and use the information gained from them, an empath can become very powerful and can help many if this gift is used and developed.

It helps to keep a dream journal. Try recalling what you dreamt about the moment you wake up. Keep the journal right near your bed so that it is easily accessible and you don't have to spend time looking for it. I say that, because we all know how quickly a dream can disappear from the mind. When we wake up it is extremely hard to remember a dream unless you have practice or a special connection with the dream world like an empath. So having access to something you can jot the details you remember down will help you not only remember but see if anything you dream about relates to your actual physical life.

Another way to develop this ability to is once again meditation. Practice keeping the mind clear and blocking out all negativity. You want to try and go to sleep as peaceful as you can. Try relaxing music or motivational talk be it tv or radio. Setting the scene before you sleep helps as well. Candles around and crystals in hand or on your wrist like a wristband. Even just by the bedside on the nightstand. Just as long as they are within reach and you can feel the power.

Having the crystals that open the crown chakra and heart chakra will allow your mind to open and be receptive to the information you may receive in the dream world and will help strengthen your mind so that you can not only get access to this information but be able to retain and use it.

Your dreams as a dream empath are everything. They are your deep spiritual connection to other realms. You are privileged to experience dreams in real time and gain information that can be used in the physical world. Granted, though empaths may receive powerful dreams and visions of things that may happen in the future and it is very hard to determine what was a dream and was a precognition.

But again, try writing down what and who you see. Write down the things you felt and read them back to yourself. Ask the universe to then guide you and let you know how these things affect your life, how the dreams pertain to reality. Sometimes we dream things that are a fractured trauma in our reality. Things that are not healed often will arise in our dreams.

From that information we can deduce that our dreams may be showing us things that we need to fix and for an empath that can be for themselves or someone that has entered their consciousness. Once someone enters their consciousness, they are able to pick up on that person or location emotions and energies and may receive information about that subject through dreams. Empaths do not have to meet or personally have been to a location for it to have entered their minds and consciousness.

The energy of either the person or location is so unique in its power depending on the events that took place there, that the empath can pick up on that energy even miles away.

Rely on these visions and dreams to guide you and compare it to the everyday life. Check for similarities and make sure your mind is open to see these things. Try and remember the conversations you have in the dream world, cross check that information to the events and situations that unfold in your life. Give this gift time to progress and indulge in research as best you can about the meaning of dreams and the powerful effect that they have on living creatures. For an empath, I recommend paying special attention to your dreams. The things you are seeing and feeling are for a reason. If you keep having a repeated dream, this may be something that you need to pay attention to because just as in physical reality, patterns and routines will be repeated until you change them.

There are dream experts and many books on the topic but the best advice I can give is rely on yourself and gift before anything else. Read and apply on the things that feel right with your spirit. Pay attention to details of your dreams and awake with a whole new meaning of reality.

PLANT EMPATHS

This topic reminds me of my grandmother. I grew up with my parents but I loved to go and see her. She had the best cooking and there were always plants around. Everywhere. Since I was about 4 years old. I remember the smell when I walked in her house in sunny California. Just beautiful. She would talk to them, water them, feed them, move them from this place to that here and there and all I remember is peace when I was there.

She had a way with plants that even as a child I understood. I wanted to be just like her when I grew up. She would tell me about every plant she had in the house, their names and their nature. Her house even felt like the plants were actually alive, and of course they are but it was different there. They all had personalities and swayed so beautifully when she walked by as if they were tune with her. The air was just soft and gentle not a toxic smell in sight. The plants kept her home protected it seemed.

As I grew older I began to do research about plants and the different kinds. Which ones are poisonous and which ones are harmless. All the usual topics I guess. But I noticed throughout time something that only experience could give me not research. It was certain peoples connection they have with plants that science cannot explain. These people feel more emotion and heart towards nature and plants than most people do. These people usually find jobs as farmers, growers, biologist, botanist, nature guides, plant & environmental analyst, tour & nature guides, etc.

There are special empaths that have divine and deep insight and higher connection with plant life of all kinds. .They can recognize the emotions of plant life and consider those feelings more than the average person does. They can feel when a plant may need to move and shift to get light, they know when they need water or nutrients outside of the day to day routine most people may have their plants on. They have the gift of knowing exactly how much a plant needs without needing instructions and manuals that may direct someone on the measurements of how much content and water it may need.

They are aware of how a plant's personality is. If it's stubborn or may be in poor health. Yes, plants and trees are actually living creatures with feelings and needs and empaths can recognize that.

Having a home full of plants can bring such comfort and calm the energy in the air. The energy in our home can vary depending on how everyone is feeling and the energies we all may have brought home. Plants can definitely help in purifying the energy along with sage and crystals. Plants are alive and they possess such a healing energy. Plants are used in medicine, in romance, in health foods, provide oxygen, and much more. They were definitely provided as an assistance to our existence. Everything is connected and needs the other to survive. The gift of communicating with plant life and nature is said to be a mythical power but where did those stories come from?

Everything comes from somewhere. As vague as that may sound, it is true. Do not overlook the deeper meanings behind things we have all come to know as "stories". Push your limits and believe in yourself, not what others might.

If you would like to test if you have this ability, first take the questionnaire below and then we will go into ways you can develop your gift!

Plant Empath Questionnaire:

- Do you have a very strong inner connection to plantlife?

- Have you always loved flowers and playing nature since childhood?

- Do you have a strong sense of empathy towards plantlife?

- Can you feel when plants are in need of water, food, etc?

- Do you love to have plants around?

- Would you work as a botanist or someone that works with plants?

- Do you enjoy learning about plant life and being in nature?

- Do you read or talk to your plants?

- Do you nurture flowers and plants?

- Do you feel a deep and spiritual feeling/communication with trees and plant life?

Now you might ask, wouldn't this pertain to any plant lover? And you would be right, yes most people who end up working in the career fields of nature and plant life are actually empaths even if they do not know it but it does not mean everyone is. Remember a lot of people on earth may have a gift but only few actually open their mind to the belief and the fact that it is real. Until that happens, the person can be as gifted as the world wishes but it will do them good if they are unaware of what they are and what they are capable of.

With this being said, hold onto the belief that this can be a real gift. In order to develop and progress yourself and this gift, be in nature as much as you can. Touch plants and talk to them. Communicate with them on a mental and enlightened level. Since you are an empath with a special connection to them, plants are able to give you the guidance that you need. They are your comfort in this life. They will provide your peace. Your environment is your safe space and plants will definitely help protect you mentally and physically as they cleanse the actual air as well. I recommend if you do not already have plants to get some and add some love and light into your house. They need light forcing you to open the windows and lift the scenes of depression tremendously.

Find different kinds of plants, take nature walks and actually touch the trees. Touching something can literally make the feeling of communication more real. It's like talking to someone on the phone and in person. The difference is major. Or a hug as opposed to just a conversation. We feel the love and emotion more when there is actually grounding involved. When we touch something, a transference of energy occurs. You are now connected to that object. Grasping the trees and actually touching the plants will help develop your ability to take care of, protect, and communicate with them.

As a plant empath you have a duty to understand, love, and safeguard plant life here on earth. They need souls like you. Life is one big circle, every creature needs the other to survive. Every living being needs the other to survive. The moon needs the sun. The stars need the moon and on and on it goes. So since we all need each other and are all here in different vessels serving our purpose, truly take part in what you believe your gift is. Find all the information you can and commune with nature. Get to know the plants and connect with them the way you were gifted to do so.

Section 12:

Physical/Medical Empaths

A *physical* and or *medical* empath is someone who can pick and feel the physical state of another person or animal. They can feel if someone is ill even if the person is not appearing to be sick. They also have release energy in a very physical way. They can actually take on the sickness of the person they are around or feeling from afar. This type of empath can feel the pain and the "health state" of another person.

Have you ever been called a "hypochondriac" or "dramatic" and may think you need to go to the doctor all the time? You may feel mysterious aches and pains with no explanation or previous medical history diagnosing any issues yet you know what you feel. These events happen randomly and are hard to determine what the source is.

A physical empath can absorb a person symptoms instead of emotions. They can feel and connect more with the body and also have a healing power. Now I am not suggesting that if an empath lays hands on you that you'll suddenly be healed but let's also not make that sound so far fetched. Long long ago, in ancient times, there were many, many believers in what would be frowned upon today. There were priests and tribes that believed in these abilities. Abilities to absorb and heal the sick. The villagers believed in oracles and prophecies. It was a much different time. People of that time believed in what could not be seen but felt. They walked more by earth and divine guidance than people do in this day and age. Overtime, many things began to be known as "witchcraft" and many were scared to be who they truly were. Afraid to ask for guidance because that would then reveal what they were capable of so seeking help became more and more dangerous to do. Now information on this is almost extinct and people over the centuries have gotten so far away from what they really are. From *who* they really are.

Now that we have a bit of back history as to why people do not openly practice this or even believe that is real, we can move on. Once again, none of these things are possible if you do not believe. And you must believe a little if you're reading this book so bravo to you! Okay, let's keep going.

Physical empaths are meant to help those of this world physically but the gift doesn't always work like that. It doesn't always work at the drop of a dime when you touch someone or walk by them. This isn't X-men. But that too is not a coincidence they had characters in those movies with the ability to shape shift, use telepathy, taking powers by touch, all those things are from actual history, as rarely talked about as they are.

Even though the gift doesn't work as a movie as I mentioned, it can be developed and it can be used. In order to discern whether or not you have absorbed someones ailment or experiencing actual pain of your own, look around if see someone you are close to is ill. If you are at work and you get a headache or sore neck out of nowhere, you may have just absorbed someone's energy. Someone may not notice an extreme difference after coming in contact with an empath, and they may be totally unaware but the empath has actually absorbed some if not a big portion of their pain and symptoms and relieved the person of their physical burdens. This happens unknowingly quite often.

Have you ever found yourself very drawn to healing, massages and trying to comfort people around you? Yes that is because the healing connection is inside of you. Not everyone has that. Everyone has a different calling, gifts, and passion. Empaths especially physical empaths are able to use their gifts for the good of the world and to benefit others. Bringing happiness and comfort to people in and of itself brings joy but most assuredly for someone that has a passion for doing so.

Physical empaths may love the job of a massage therapist, physical trainer, gym trainer, nurse, dietician, doctors, pharmacists and veterinarians. These careers involve healing and diagnosing problems and illness in the human body. If you are someone that absorbs others physical illness and symptoms and have a vast interest in healing others pain, I recommend these fields.

There is also starting support groups and talking with others that have this physical connection and take pointers on how they cope with and develop it. You have the power to absorb and heal the physical state of being. Use this power in a world that is full of darkness to add light and happiness into someone's life.

EMOTIONAL EMPATH

An emotional empath is not the same as an emotional person. Though you may feel emotions, and every human does, unless they are a sociopath, every human displays them differently. Each emotion that has a different energy attached to it.

Hate - Toxic Energy

Love - Positive Energy

Spite - Toxic Energy

Jealousy - Toxic Energy

Romance - Positive Energy

Happiness - Positive Energy

Sadness - Low Vibrating Energy

Nervousness - Middle-grade confusing/foggy Energy that causes imbalance

To an emotional empath, this is exactly what we see. We see energy as clear as the hand in front of your face. We can feel that energy in a very raw form that we can begin to display physically if it is too much for us to handle. It may come out or release itself in physical form perhaps like illness because though you cannot "see" energy it is very real and flows through the body of an empath like water.

An emotional empath can absorb the emotions of those they are around and anyone that comes in contact with their consciousness. Someone can enter the consciousness by several means. By just watching something on tv, by seeing them in the paper, by hearing their name but never met them. Another way is what I call the "energy travel wave". The energy can be so powerful within a person or situation regardless of location that an empath can pick it up miles and miles away.

If someone that we are around is sad, we may also feel sad. Not the typical empathetic "just trying to be nice" sadness that some people get and you can't fault them for that. Not everyone is deeply attached to every human being emotionally and feels these emotions. An emotional empath will literally feel the pain and know exactly what that person is going through as if they are in their shoes. They can relate on a whole other level to a subject or place.

Emotions and vibrations are what ground the empath to this particular gift. It is not foresight or physical connection but emotions, body language, and the energy field surrounding someone or something. All these things tell the empath exactly what they need to know in order to either help someone or stay away from them. Emotions and vibes are extremely important to pay attention to for an empath. It means their mental sanity. See, having the gift of absorbing energy and emotion is not always buttercups and kisses. It can be draining. It can be exhausting and rough on the physical state after much time of not healing yourself or recuperating from absorbing others energy.

Without a filter or net to catch and decipher the energy you want to let in, you absorb it all. The toxic, the sad, the negative, the good, and the bad. So this is when the use of crystals and being informed comes in handy and to great benefit. For an emotional empath, the **Lepidolite** grounding stone is excellent in its power of lessening the feelings of stress, anxiety, and fear that we may absorb. It is associated with the heart and brow chakras and helps heal the emotional body. It is also a great filter helping you discern which feelings of anger and anxiety or yours or someone else's.

The **Hematite** crystal is another amazing grounding stone that keeps you grounded to the earth and deflect and ward off harmful energies. For an emotional empath, a stone such as this and others like it are crucial. Since you have the power to take energy from others you want to be careful of any energies that could harm you and your state of mind. Emotion is energy in motion and it is heavily based on the intent and inner soul of the person. Their actions will define the type of energy that they carry. Their emotions, which in so many words are a display of energy in physical form, will also define the type of energy the subject carries.

It helps to pay attention to two key things for this gift. Your gut or intuition and your ability to see past what meets the human eye. As an emotional empath you can see past someone's lies, you are able to see through a person not just the surface. You read body language much differently than most people. You also see the "aura" or the overall energy surrounding someone. There is a distinct energy surrounding every person on earth. Carrying the reaffirming stones and crystals will aid you in the belief that you have help in the universe and that you are grounded to the earth giving you that need connection in order to enhance your abilities.

Use these things to develop and heighten your skills and see the new things you can learn.

GEOMANTIC EMPATH

Have you found yourself in a location and you either felt like you've been there before or as if you were very uncomfortable? Have you found yourself really happy in certain environments for no apparent reason and you've never been there? You may be geomantic empath that also has different names in the spiritual world that has changed over time. This particular type of empath has the gift of being attached and connected to places on the earth and in the universe.

They feel a deep connection to certain places and may be fond of sacred stones, historical sites, and other places of a "sacred" power. When you go somewhere or read about a place and time in history you may feel the emotions of that location and the events that took place there. You'll feel the energy and emotions that were going on.

There were practices long ago, of women using their powers touching their hand on the ground from palm to fingers, and absorbing the information from that location. This would assist villages when it came to approaching storms, enemies and hidden information that the gifted would try and use their powers to find.

Geomantic empaths are highly attuned to the natural world. They are repulsed by the sight of trees being cut down or the earth being damaged. They appreciate landmarks and see them from a different perspective than most. They understand and truly feel the energy behind the structure. Some people see a landmark or visit a sacred site and they'll take pictures, enjoy themselves, and leave but for an empath, it is much different and a much deeper connection happening when an empath walks on certain grounds.

Have you walked into a place and felt as if you knew something bad had happened there? That feeling some people get when they walk through haunted houses or graveyards is not mistake and believe it or not, not everyone has that "eerie" feeling. For them it's just a house that something bad happened inside of, and for them it's just a graveyard. Must be nice sometimes because for an empath it is not that. We feel the energy of what took place, we know that their are restless souls there when we walk inside of a graveyard but the ordinary eye cannot see this. When I go to or drive by a graveyard I don't have a necessarily scared feeling but I've always felt as if they weren't really dead. For some reason I can't walk on or near a place like that without feeling more than just the fact that it's a graveyard. It's so intense and has always been tough for me to explain. I cry, that's for sure anytime I see one or I see a hearse and I've never met those people.

This gift can be developed by going to different places and closing your eyes. Mediating briefly and thinking closely about the things you are feeling and experiencing. Try to determine if you are seeing and feeling an event from the past or if you've seen that location in your dreams. What energies do you feel? Positive or negative?

Asking yourself these things will awaken your mind and with that you can have a receptive vessel in order to see things and events in that location with a clear mind.

For this you want to make sure you have a calm and clear mind, blocking out negativity and you want to protect your energies. A great stone to use for that is the *Black Tourmaline* crystal. This is a protective and shielding crystal. It helps protect the purity of your space so if you want to practice your unique ability, this will help keep out any unwanted energetic mental interference.

The *Amethyst* crystal comes in many different beautiful colors and shapes. It is a natural stress reliever that encourages inner strength and peace. It stimulates the crown chakra and greatly aids in meditation. The more open yet calmer the mind is, the better it is for you to use and develop your ability.

Being in and around nature as much as possible and visiting places with a sacred history will allow you to give your gifts a chance to flourish. Be involved as you can, keep records of the places you go along with the places you see in your dreams and see if you can bring your abilities into reality.

SECTION 13: ENDING

INFORMATION & TIPS

Just like a superhero or a villain you have the choice to use your powers for good or "bad".

At the end of the day, being an empath is not a choice so it doesn't matter who you are but I guess it comes down to your personality. What type of person you are. Just because someone is an empath does not automatically make them "angels" and people that walk on water. If you are a person that has empathic abilities but your intentions are of an ill nature, you will poison the pureness of your gift.

In order to develop your gifts, dive into the things you experience. Seek out others that have had similar feelings and events happen in their lives. Research and read books on the topic. Knowledge is freedom and power. Having the information you need will assist you on your journey to enlightenment. It will help guide you, teach you new practices and techniques to help calm your mind, and allow you to see that you are not alone in the things you are dealing with.

Empaths are a gift to a harsh world. This world can be cruel and without empathic, understanding people, it would be much worse. Imagine if everyone was self-centered, self-serving, and prideful? What if everyone only worried about themselves and neglected their family, friends and children? What would the world be? Much more complicated than it is now. Empaths have a responsibility, a duty here on earth to protect, save, and heal the people in this world. To soften the blow of a hard and difficult life. To make the journey on this earth a little more soothing and peaceful. Now of course we're not perfect as empaths, we have to learn ourselves, realize what we and our purpose before we can help anyone. We must heal ourselves to be able to help someone else.

It can take time to fully understand what you are capable of. But have patience with yourself and continue to learn all you can. In time, things will come together and you will indeed find your calling in life. As mentioned in chapter 3, there are several career fields well suited for empaths. Starting your own business in massage therapy or finding a job in that field might be a great suggestion. Jobs that involve healing and helping others. Nurses, home health aids and wellness coaches are all wonderful choices as well that involve helping others and brightening their day.

You can also create support groups and online videos that help others and it creates a forum for discussion on this topic. In doing so, you are opening the doors of knowledge and you can discover things and activities that you may not have tried that someone else can offer. You can find friends and like minded people to share your journey with as well. But at days end, your gift and what you choose to do with it is entirely up to you. What will you do with yours? How will impact your world and those around you? Positively or negatively.

There are many different experiences in the world and all could be described as "impossible" but they happen. Those cases of people getting Hulk like strength and able to lift a car, people that have been able to tell the future with no cards or a crystal ball, cases where people have literally healed someone they hugged or touched. But since those things are so rare to actually hear about especially mainstream, people have a hard time tapping to those abilities.

An ability and a calling are very closely related. If you have an extreme passion or are very drawn to certain practices and ways, you may have an unknown and suppressed ability. If you are drawn heavily to nature then perhaps you have the unique gift of communicating with nature, plants and animals as an earth or animal empath. If you love healing and taking care of people and you genuinely feel their emotions, you may be an emotional and or physical empath.

The things that you feel calling to you, answer them. The positive things of course. A gift that needs shaping but it is one of the hardest to pinpoint to a science is an intuitive, precognitive empath. That again, is the ability to see future events be it through dreams or visions while you are awake. It is ties in with the ability to touch things or see a person or location and be able to see and feel the energy of the past, present, and future. As difficult as this may sound, it is very possible. If you are gifted with the talent, then you are already ahead. You are already gaining divine insight you just may need to nurture it. I am not aware of how to learn how to see the future or the past, I can only tell you from a place of honesty and experience that I only can further improve upon this gift because I already possess it, I cannot teach anyone to do this. This book is for the purposes of learning to develop what it already there and I hope it helps a great deal.

As you progress in life and come across new information apply it. Apply it and use it so that you do not have to go through the unnecessary struggles that your gift is there to guide you through. Everyone has a job. A purpose. I personally do not think we are here on earth for no apparent reason. Have you ever looked at life and realized that it comes with a lot of lessons? As if that's what it's all about? Have you looked around and realized that every person on earth has a different talent? A different and unique personality? Yes, no two people not even twins are the same exact person. No soul is like the other. Every plant is different, every piece of sand and soil is unique. Every star, as many as there are, is unique.

The conclusion I draw from these differences and the unique way everything is positioned on earth and created is that everything and every person is and has been here in this universe for a reason. Find your reason, find your purpose, and if you have an ability it won't take long for it to surface. We are in a time of a massive energy shift and a real awakening. People are coming into great knowledge and are applying it to their lives. Stay grounded, humble, and connected to the earth. It is your home. Embrace the universe, the sun is every creatures' energy source.

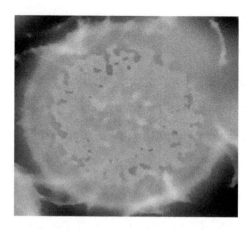

Spend time in nature and less with electronics. You are a biological but spiritual being that needs the life and energy of others in order to survive. We need food, which is energy. We need water, which is also energy. Every human being needs the sun and the plants for oxygen and energy. Connect with these sources and the positive energy from other people and live a bright and vibrant life.

Life is not meant to be hard no matter routine and exhausting it may be. We get lost in the day to day shuffle, the keep of the bills, and the expectations of society, family and friends. Those distractions mislead you from the true purpose in life. From your own path. So of course, yes, take care of life's obligations but do not neglect yourself, your happiness and your purpose along the way.

Take time out for yourself and practice meditation and yoga. Create the environment you want and need to survive in a peaceful state of mind. Allow only those that bring comfort and happiness into your life. Block out all negativity and unnecessary energy.

This goes towards television, media, social media, toxic relationships, negative family and friends and so on. Watch things that will bring you motivation and push you to be a better person. Find practices online and in books that provide information on raising your awareness and assist you on your path of enlightenment.

Being an empath keeps you in touch with your spiritual side at all times. You feel emotions and things that are hard to explain to someone that is not involved or heavily interested in the spiritual and divine realm. These emotions, thoughts and feelings can be overwhelming without a place to release this energy and without guidance. Rely on the grounding effects of your crystals. Rely on their shielding and reassuring effects. Crystals contain magnetic and powerful energy that is designed to help us here on earth, where they are formed. They help shield you from bad energy, feelings of anxiety and anger that you may have absorbed from someone else, and they provide feelings of strength, motivation and boldness. There are so many more healing and energetic effects that stones and crystals possess. Find the ones that work for you, your gift, and the circumstances that you may need them for. Each has a purpose and unique affect.

Lastly, I would like to end this by wishing you well on your journey. Listen to your inner soul and rely heavily on your intuition. You are capable of anything that you put your mind to and if you are blessed with abilities to bring light and happiness into this world, do not hesitate. Do not doubt yourself. Doubt is the biggest killer of dreams. Believe in yourself and you will succeed greatly with the empathetic gifts you were given.

Lightning Source UK Ltd.
Milton Keynes UK
UKHW021132010223
416301UK00015B/933